Travel

Undiscovered
Islands of the
U.S. and Canadian
West Coast

P

Undiscovered Islands of the U.S. and Canadian West Coast

Linda Lancione Moyer
and
Burl Willes

John Muir Publications
Santa Fe, New Mexico

An RDR Syndicate Book
John Muir Publications, P.O. Box 613, Santa Fe, NM 87504

© 1992 by Linda Lancione Moyer and Burl Willes
Cover and maps © 1992 by John Muir Publications
All rights reserved.
Printed in the United States of America

First edition. First printing October 1991

Library of Congress Cataloging-in-Publication Data

Moyer, Linda.
    Undiscovered islands of the U.S. and Canadian west coast / Linda
Lancione Moyer and Burl Willes.   —   1st ed.
        p.   cm.
    ISBN 1-56261-013-9
    1. Pacific Coast (North America)—Description and travel—Guide
-books.   2. Islands—Pacific Coast (North America)—Description
and travel—Guide-books.   I. Willes, Burl, 1941-   .   II. Title.
F851.M93   1992
917.904'33—dc20   91-31147
                                                                    CIP

Distributed to the book trade by:
W. W. Norton & Company, Inc.
New York, New York

Illustrations: Sally Blakemore
Cover art: Holly Wood
Maps: Holly Wood
Photos: Barbara Stross, Linda Lancione Moyer, Burl Willes,
    Sandy McCulloch, National Park Service
Typography: Copygraphics, Inc.
Printer: Malloy Lithographing, Inc.

CONTENTS

CONTENTS

ACKNOWLEDGMENTS

We have many people to thank, above all, Barbara Stross for her assistance with Oregon and Alaska and Christina Rajaratnam for the Gulf Islands. We are also grateful to Elaine Eisenstadt for her observations on Petersburg. Thank you also to Peter Beren, Roger Rapoport, and the staff of John Muir Publications for their help.

INTRODUCTION

B url's book on the Caribbean islands drew sighs of envy from his friends, and the book we wrote together on the Mediterranean islands brought disbelief at our good fortune. This time, when we announced we were writing about islands along the Pacific Coast, we drew blank stares, then "Are there any?" or bad jokes about Alcatraz. Indeed, there are, most of them clustered in the Pacific Northwest. In Alaska, British Columbia, and Washington, we had an embarrassment of riches to select from. In Oregon and northern California, we dipped into the coastal bays, rivers, and deltas to round out our assortment before proceeding down the coast to the Channel group.

What ties together the remote, rough and ready islands of Alaska, at one extreme, and the sun-kissed tropicality of Catalina, at the other? Accessibility: most of the islands that we selected are no more than ninety minutes from shore, and some are considerably closer to shore. Another similarity is each island's contrast to the nearby mainland; to use our favorite example, the swift leap from the crowded freeways of Los Angeles to the unpeopled areas of Catalina is mind-boggling.

As the pace and problems of urban life intensify, there is more and more need for this kind of easy, peaceful escape. Everybody likes to get away from it all, but at the same time, no one wants to have to go very far. In this book, we offer a range of close-to-coast possibilities for the nature lover, the sophisticate, and the sun worshiper.

But, you ask, won't an increase in tourism spoil these places? There are several factors that weigh against that possibility. First, the island communities themselves (or in the case of the unpopulated islands we've included, the agencies that protect them) are vigilant against environmental damage or unchecked development. Although they accept that some change is inevitable and often welcome an influx of vacationers as an economic boon, they know what they've got and want to keep it that way. Second, limited water and ferry service also contain growth. Third, facilities are limited, there are no major tourist attractions at these locales, and it takes a little extra effort and planning to cross the water, all factors that mitigate against mass tourism.

For the first time, we have included islands that are uninhabited and have no hotel facilities, notably, the Channel Islands and Angel Island in California and Sauvie and Ross islands in Oregon. This is in keeping with our intent to suggest places of escape and respite, even if only for a day, from life on the mainland. Where appropriate, we have suggested excursions and places to eat and stay on the nearby shore.

Whether you visit these islands for a day, a weekend, or a week or more, we hope you'll find them as lovely as we did, leave them as lovely as you found them, and return to shore with a more peaceful heart.

ALASKA

From the misty Pribilof Islands in the Bering Sea to the massive glaciers, fjords, and wooded islands of the Southeast Alaska panhandle, the scenery of the 49th U.S. state is majestic and unspoiled. There are literally thousands of islands for the visitor to explore, but nearly all are uninhabited and inaccessible except by private boat or floatplane.

The two inhabited Pribilof Islands, Saint Paul and Saint George, are magical destinations for nature enthusiasts. The battered coastline of Saint George offers refuge to 2.5 million seabirds representing 200 species that nest there each summer. A million fur seals swim ashore to breed and raise their young on these remote islands. Arctic wildflowers shimmer with color on those few long days of brilliant sunshine in July and August.

We recommend the Pribilofs, the Aleutians, and foggy Kodiak Island for the avid nature lover willing to undertake the effort and substantial expense to get there. But for those who want to savor the unspoiled yet amazingly accessible Alaska, we have chosen two totally different Southeast Alaska islands: Annette and Mitkof.

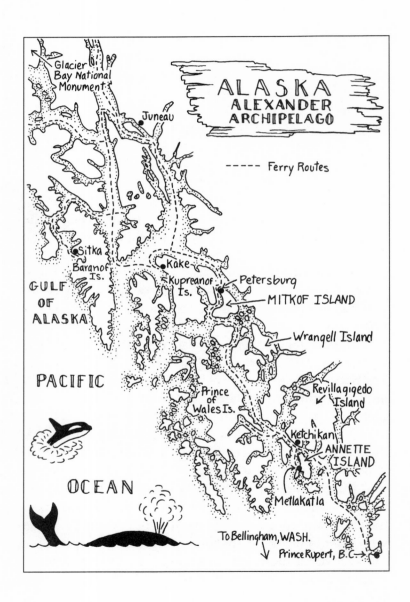

Annette is less than an hour by ferry from Ketchikan, or the first stop out of Wrangell if you are taking the ferry north through the Inside Passage. It is of special interest because it is autonomously governed by the Tsimshian tribe.

Farther north, through the most spectacular section of the Inside Passage, lies Mitkof, an island so close to Kupreanof—its larger neighbor—that at times the ferry literally brushes against the densely wooded landscape of both islands at once. Petersburg is a charming hidden seacoast town of Norwegian heritage in an idyllic setting of mountains and sea at the north end of the island.

Late spring and early summer are the best times to go anywhere in Alaska. The visitor need go no farther than these surprisingly close islands to savor the vastness, solitude, and beauty that make Alaska one of the most exhilarating travel destinations in the world.

Annette

In a state rich in Native American culture and heritage, Annette Island is remarkable for being Alaska's only Indian reservation. It was never sold to the federal government as most of the other Native American lands were. Tribal traditions, dedication to religious ideals, access to modern media, and dependence on the tools of technology all blend in shaping the way of life on this intriguing island.

Annette lies southwest of Ketchikan and is an easy day excursion from there. The island's town, Metlakatla, has about 2,400 permanent residents, 1,600 of whom are Native Americans. With rare exceptions, there is no higher authority than the local government. The tribal council, under the leadership of the mayor, operates a strong, independent democracy. The tribe owns all land and provides building lots and housing for its members. Non-natives lease apartments, homes, and offices. Businesses on the island must be owned and operated by a member of the tribe.

Metlakatla has the only legal fish traps for salmon in Alaska, an acknowledgment of the Indians' right to fish in their traditional way. The fishermen employ a long net as a wall, forcing the fish into large wood-and-net traps. These devices are so efficient that only four may be used every other day for a two-and-a-half-month season so that enough fish are allowed through to spawn.

During the summer months, the harbor is jammed with boats, and a cannery handles the bounty of the fishing fleet. The fish cannery usually needs a large crew of summer workers and frequently has to import seasonal laborers. The Annette Hemlock Sawmill is the other major source of employment on the island. Both businesses are owned by the tribe, and every member receives an annual dividend from profits.

Metlakatla Power and Light is also owned by the community. Two hydroelectric generators are turned by a 360-foot head of water from Purple Lake as it empties into the ocean. A third generator depends on the water falling from Chester Lake into Metlakatla's bay, close to the ferry landing. A diesel-run generator responds to sudden energy demands, especially from the sawmill.

Metlakatla is a small, friendly town. People are curious about visitors and extraordinarily generous with help,

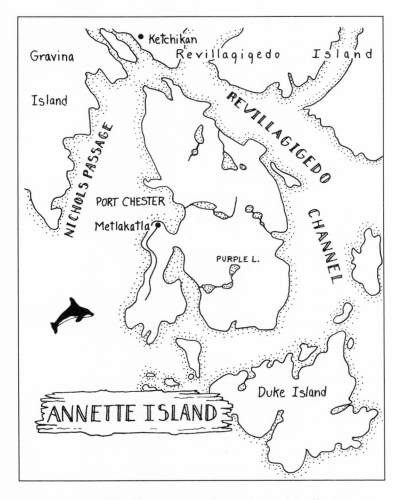

directions, and information. A few minutes' walk takes you through the entire business district, which has one bank, a few stores, and no traffic lights. The Village Store carries some beautiful jewelry made by local artists and an astonishing choice of other goods as well, from microwave popcorn-on-the-cob to homeopathic medicines, post-cards, and make-up.

The community traces its history back to 1887 when a Church of England missionary, William Duncan, following a disagreement with his superiors, moved here from British Columbia with several hundred Tsimshian Indians. In 1891, Congress granted reservation status and title to the island. The Duncan Museum displays turn-of-the-century photographs of Metlakatla as well as the personal artifacts of William Duncan. During the tourist season, the museum is open from 10:00 a.m. to 5:00 p.m., Monday through Friday. Admission is $1.00.

The traditional Tribal Loghouse, a relatively new and impressive log building, is located near the harbor just behind the town's single totem pole. The building serves as a community hall where dances, salmon bakes, and other local celebrations are held. This is also the location of the community library as well as an exhibit of local Native American painting and carvings and two models of the fish traps, which are an invention of the tribe.

Near the outskirts of town, dozens of rusting, dented quonset huts recall a time when thousands lived and worked here during World War II, when the airport was a refueling station for planes being shipped north to the Aleutian Islands. Today, most of the impressive buildings at the airport are deserted, although one is still used for nightly big-stake bingo games. Another building with a small weather balloon hangar nearby houses the federal weather station. If you are inclined, you can watch the balloon's release twice a day, at 3:00 a.m. and 3:00 p.m.

Weather reports are made on Alaska time. Metlakatla is on Pacific time, which is one hour ahead.

Wildlife and outdoors enthusiasts could explore the island for years without tiring. Even though Metlakatlans have fishing rights to 3,000 feet offshore, the waters remain bountiful. There are twenty-five kinds of rock fish, shrimp, crab, cockles, butter clams, mussels, oysters, salmon, and abalone and an occasional geoduck. Eulachon, or candle fish, are valued for their oil, which is used like butter. Dried, the whole fish burns easily. Metlakatla is on the migrating route of whales and porpoises, and sea otters live in the bay and around the island.

Hunters follow deer into the mountains, and, in turn, rescue parties look for lost hunters every year. There are wolves but no bears on Annette. It's easy to spot bald eagles, especially around town, where trash attracts scavengers.

The beaches are mixed sand, gravel, and boulders, lined with scattered driftwood and trees. East of town, the

BARBARA STROSS

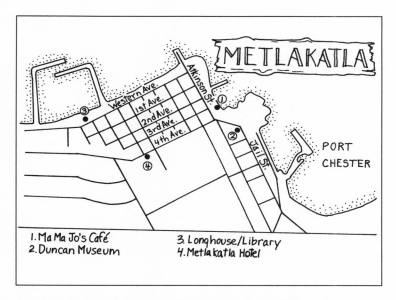

1. Ma Ma Jo's Café
2. Duncan Museum
3. Longhouse/Library
4. Metlakatla Hotel

cemetery's headstones and grave markers follow the coastline for a quarter mile, broken by the newly completed Pioneer Park. Set in sparse forest and opening on a beach brilliant in the sun, the park has plenty of picnic tables and barbecue pits.

Point Davis is at the end of one of countless unimproved roads beyond the airport. With spectacular natural vistas and plentiful clamming, it's a good base for exploring Annette's shoreline. Closer to town, the three-mile Purple Lake trail offers a steep, rugged, and beautiful hike. The island air is always fresh, perfect for enjoying the spectacular view of forests on still-snowy mountains and the endless ocean horizon.

Between the beaches and the mountains, much of the lower land is muskeg, a thick layer of water-soaked peat and rotting wood above almost impervious clay and gravel glacial till. With Alaska's relatively cool summers and ample rainfall, the muskeg is freckled with standing pools. Its wet, acid soil supports a variety of bog-loving plants whose summer flowering is radiant. The stunted shore pine is about the only tree, and even that rarely grows more than fifteen feet high in 300 to 400 years. Rotting trees, typical of "muskeg kill," are part of the landscape.

To the right of the road heading from town toward the airport, there is an unusual series of hillocks clustered together in one lumpy hill that is noticeably different from the surrounding muskeg. The soil and boulders here are quite yellow, giving it the name Yellow Hill. At the top, another wonderful view follows an easy, cross-country climb.

Many visitors choose to schedule Annette as a day trip from Ketchikan, but the abundant hiking, fishing, and beachcombing invite a more leisurely visit for those who prefer unguided, independent, and unhurried adventures.

BARBARA STROSS

BARBARA STROSS

HOW TO GET THERE

By boat: Metlakatla is now served four times a week from Ketchikan by the ferry *Aurora*. On Saturday, the ferry stops there twice, making it possible to do a day trip from Ketchikan. The trip takes one hour and costs $15.00 each way.

By air: Alaska Airlines has nonstop service to Ketchikan three times a day from Seattle with easy connections from Ketchikan to Metlakatla. Taquan Air Service also has four round-trips daily. The flight takes fifteen minutes and costs $52.00 round-trip. Temsko Airlines has several daily flights to Metlakatla from Ketchikan, $25.00 each way.

WHERE TO STAY

Metlakatla Hotel, Box 670, Metlakatla, AK, (907) 886-5280. These accommodations reflect the personal vision and taste of owners Dale and Edith Olin. Italian marble floors and splendidly appointed suites are designed for guests who enjoy both comfort and luxury. The Olins will meet guests at the floatplane dock. The ferry landing is a short taxi ride from town. Moderate to expensive.

WHERE TO EAT

Ma Ma Jo's, on the waterfront near the cannery, is one of the only restaurants, and while its prices reflect the added expense of ferrying food from Ketchikan, the view of ocean, islands, and icy peaks is a grand compensation. For fast food, try the burger stand or the ice-cream parlor. The just-opened *Metlakatla Hotel* offers a brand-new dining spot with a less casual atmosphere.

Mitkof

From the plane between Wrangell and Petersburg, it looks like the water is strewn with large chunks of polystyrene. But more and more pieces steadily appear, far too many to be local debris. Suddenly, this totally unexpected sight makes perfect sense. Below our plane's descent path, glaciers have dropped countless fragments, filling the surrounding waters with tiny broken icebergs. Le Conte Glacier, set in a deep canyon at the head of Le Conte Bay, twenty-five miles east of Petersburg, is the most southerly tidewater glacier on the coast and one of the most active. The lake at its base is often carpeted with floating bergs and ''bergy bits.'' Alaska is impressive.

Often passed over by large cruise ships unable to nav-

LECONTE GLACIER

Petersburg
← Sandy Beach

Ravens
Roost Trail

Kupreanof

Island

Falls Creek
Fish Ladder

Blind Slough
Rec. Area

Three
Lakes Trails

Crystal Lake
Fish Hatchery

Ohmer Creek
Campground

Sumner Strait
Campground

BLIND SLOUGH

MITKOF ISLAND

Wrangell

igate the narrow channels, Petersburg is a charming town and makes an ideal base to explore the hiking trails and parks on Mitkof Island.

Petersburg is one of the prettiest seacoast communities on the shores of the Pacific. The spick-and-span tidiness, the ordered beauty of scores of white fishing boats moored in the harbor, and the open, island-dotted seascape give the visitor a sense of soothing, purposeful calm.

Petersburg is not a typical Alaskan tent-and-log-cabin boomtown. Founded in 1897 by Peter Buschmann and settled by fellow Norwegians, it is the youngest community in the Panhandle, yet it has the largest home-based halibut fleet in Alaska. The spirit of Norway is very much alive here. Some buildings are decorated in the traditional flowery *rosemaling* style with handpainted borders of flowers and curlicues. Norwegian Independence Day—May 17—is the occasion of a festival that includes games, dancing, and a huge potluck dinner.

This tiny settlement is one of the friendliest places we have ever visited. Each person we passed on the street greeted us. A walk around this extremely prosperous town begins at the thriving harbor, which extends along the waterfront the length of Petersburg. Here are the canneries that fuel the economy of the community; they are so busy in summer that seasonal workers must be housed in a tent city near the airport. In fact, the fishing is so rich that the limit for the recent halibut season was reached in twelve hours. Northwest of the main dock there are moorages for a multitude of fishing boats, family vessels, and travelers. One parking lot is designated an RV staging area, with an eight-hour limit. Another allows fourteen-day parking for long-term harbor users. On the other side of this multiuse dock are the floatplane dock and the Coast Guard and state ferry docks.

At the Harbor Master's office, open early and late, people on duty are friendly and very helpful if you need directions or have questions. The same building, on the edge of the main dock, has public showers and rest rooms, and all seven pages of Petersburg's phone book are posted on the

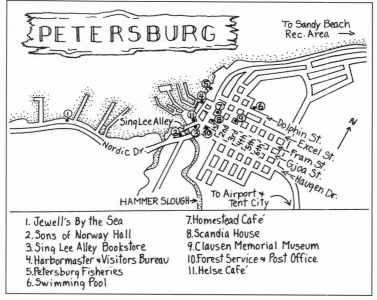

1. Jewell's By the Sea
2. Sons of Norway Hall
3. Sing Lee Alley Bookstore
4. Harbormaster & Visitors Bureau
5. Petersburg Fisheries
6. Swimming Pool
7. Homestead Café
8. Scandia House
9. Clausen Memorial Museum
10. Forest Service & Post Office
11. Helse Café

wall next to a large city map alongside the public phone booth. The same map, whose key locates major points of interest and public buildings, is posted at the main bus stop and the museum.

A walk down Sing Lee Alley, which follows the tidal area, leads to Hammer Slough. Clusters of weathered homes and boathouses suspended on pillars above the shoreline share space with old boats, crab pots, and nets—the whole scene mirrored in the still water. This is our choice for the most photogenic spot in town.

Sing Lee Alley Books, a terrific bookstore just behind the library in Sing Lee Alley, has a large selection of new and interesting hardcovers, paperbacks, cards, and posters. You can have lunch and start your book at one of several

BARBARA STROSS

picnic tables in the big yard outside.

In summer, when the glacier chunks in the bay disappear and night lasts only a few short hours, the residents of Petersburg take advantage of the long days to garden like mad, producing foxglove, delphinium, columbine, and other showy flowers. The four city blocks are graced with hanging baskets of fuchsias. An abundance of eagles also decorate the city streets. They can be seen perched atop trees and lamp posts until it is time for them to cruise out over the cove for a meal of fish.

If it's summer, and not yet 5:00 p.m., you can get tea or fresh brewed coffee (latte, espresso, etc.) at Helse, the nearby natural food store, and walk out on the dock. From a seat at one of the sidewalk café-like tables, it's easy to watch the boats returning from a day's fishing or setting out on an afternoon sail.

Most businesses and shops are no more than a block or two off North or South Nordic (main street). Artists can buy supplies and see the work of several local potters and painters at Jewell's By The Sea. There are two other art stores downtown. Husfliden, upstairs in the Sons of Norway Hall, which was built in 1912 and is on the National Register of Historic Places, stocks Norwegian handicrafts, art supplies, jewelry, and small gift items. Berthiel's, on the main street, has a nice collection of locally made and imported clothes, jewelry, and glass.

Take F Street off Nordic Drive to the Clausen Memorial Museum, a tribute to the fishing abundance that created this active port. The museum contains local artifacts, Norwegian costumes, and a king salmon weighing over 126 pounds (one of the largest ever caught).

In town, there are also facilities for swimming. At Petersburg High School is the Roundtree Swimming Pool, which charges a small fee for use of the pool, showers, and lockers.

A walk "out on the road," as they say in these small Alaskan towns, leads to some beautiful homes overlooking the bay and glaciers on the other side. Walkers can start at Eagles Roost Park at the east end of the business district and walk for miles on the beach. Heavy shoes are advised. Going out of town, the shoreline is more than ankle-deep in broken glass, some polished completely smooth, other pieces still sharp. Shards of every shape and color from every country seem to have assembled on this spot. A little farther on, the beach is suddenly plated with pieces of scrap metal.

Beyond this stretch, formerly a dump, is Sandy Beach,

which is true to its name and the only one on the island. It's a scenic cove with sweeping views of other islands, migrating whales, and the mainland across the waterway. When heavy tides wash out the sand, city trucks deliver a new supply. Looking up, you may spot several bald eagles' nests on exposed treetop branches. Nesting begins in late March, and chicks, usually two to a nest, hatch out from mid- to late May.

On the other side of Sandy Beach, a mile-long boardwalk across the muskeg leads to Fredrick Point. The view of the muskeg bloom and its incomparable array of colors unfolding on a muted background allows the opportunity to study the complex, rare, and very delicate terrain without doing it damage.

When you return to the Fredrick Point trailhead, which is near the dump, you will find that the gulls, ravens, and crows are as raucous as parrots in a tropical jungle. Eagles, three to a tree, make themselves heard, too, while bears are encountered frequently enough to merit several posted warning signs along the road. Canadian geese, usually in pairs, are noisy also but prefer to feed on the muskeg.

Headed back to town, you can use a short boardwalk across the muskeg from Twelfth to Tenth and Exel. Two comfortable benches along the walk make it easy to admire the view, listen to the birds, or just doze in the sun.

For further outdoor possibilities, inquire at the Petersburg Ranger Station for the Tongass National Forest, on the second floor of the federal building above the post office on N. Nordic. This national forest encompasses 16.8 million acres, or more than 73 percent of all the land in southeastern Alaska. Its name comes from the Tongass clan of

BARBARA STROSS

BARBARA STROSS

Tlingit Indians, who lived on an island at the southern end of the forest. The ranger station has good maps of Mitkof and the entire district, which includes Kupreanof, Kulu, other small islands, and parts of the mainland as well. If you want to visit remote areas, ask about reserving one of the nineteen federal recreation cabins in the Petersburg Ranger District. Accessible only by floatplane or boat, the cabins let you escape the city and share unclouded streams and uncluttered forests with trout, salmon, moose, deer, goats, bears, and grouse. Leave internal parasites out of the adventure, though: boil your drinking water.

The Supervisor's Office for Tongass National Forest, Stikine Area, on Twelfth Street just off Jaugen, has more maps and lots of information about the fish, wildlife, water, soil, plants, timber, and terrain of this region.

To see how today's fishing is done, visit the Petersburg Fisheries, one of Alaska's most advanced fish plants. Fish enthusiasts will also want to visit the Crystal Lake Fish Hatchery and the Falls Creek fish ladder at Mile 13.7 on the Mitkof Highway. The ladder, which allows the pink salmon and coho to bypass the falls, is best seen in August and early September. When you're tired of looking at fish, stop in at the Trumpeter Swan Observatory for a look at these elegant birds.

There is good cross-country skiing not far from town. Helicopter surveys now in progress are the first step in a plan to develop a downhill ski area on Mitkof.

Kake, on Kupreanof, is well worth a side trip from Petersburg. It is the traditional home of the Kake tribe of the Tlinglit Indians and the site of the largest totem pole in Alaska.

Wherever you are on Mitkof, the spectacular, sharply defined peaks on the mainland and forested slopes on Kupreanof Island just across the straits, are never out of sight. It's a delight to look around and a special treat when snow showers out of the almost-clear blue sky.

The cruise up or down the Inside Passage, especially the twists and turns of Wrangell Narrows between Mitkof and Kupreanof, is an unforgettable introduction to one of the most spectacular and powerful terrains on our planet.

HOW TO GET THERE

By boat: The State Marine Ferry operates from Juneau or Ketchikan to Petersburg. From Bellingham, Washington, to Ketchikan the one-way adult fare is $154.00 for the 36-

hour voyage. From Prince Rupert to Ketchikan, it's only six hours by ferry and $32.00. Ketchikan to Petersburg is nine hours and $45.00. Petersburg to Juneau is just under eight hours and costs $42.00. Reservations are required on all ferries. Telephone (800) 624-0066.

By air: There are several flights a day from Ketchikan to Petersburg on Alaska Airlines, Ketchikan Air, and Temsco Airlines. The flying time is 90 minutes, with one stop in Wrangell, and the fare is $105.00 one way. Wings of Alaska, Ketchikan Air, and Alaska Island Air offer service from Petersburg to Kake, 20 minutes and $30.00 each way. There are nonstop flights from Juneau to Petersburg on Alaska Airlines and Wings of Alaska, a 65-minute flight that costs $100.00 one way, less on a round-trip 14-day advance purchase.

Getting there is half the fun on these Alaska flights, which allow you to survey the magnificently contoured landscape stretching beyond sight on every side.

WHERE TO STAY

Jewell's By The Sea, P.O. Box 1662, Petersburg, AK 99833, (907) 772-4820 or (907) 772-3620. This is a real find. Jewell's house, a bed and breakfast with three bedrooms, rests on pilings over the water. Windows in the kitchen, dining room, and living room have an uninterrupted view of mountains, boats, ducks, and bald eagles. Jewell's goal is "to help make your stay in Alaska memorable." She tries her best to fulfill your needs by picking you up from the airport or ferry, arranging charters for fishing or sightseeing, and cooking a hearty full breakfast complete with waffle or hash browns, cereal, and fruit. Inexpensive.

Scandia House, 110 Nordic Drive, Petersburg, AK 99833, (907) 772-4281. This 85-year-old hotel, centrally located near restaurants and across the street from the boat harbor, has been remodeled and provides visitors with inexpensive rooms without bath and moderately priced rooms with bath. Some kitchen units are available. The hotel also has boat and car rentals. The owners are very accommodating about picking up guests at the ferry, which sometimes arrives at 2:00 a.m. Moderate.

WHERE TO EAT

Rey Restaurant, across from the ferry terminal, has everything from prime rib to fresh jumbo shrimp. *Petersburg Fish Company*, on Nordic Drive near the ferry terminal, is highly recommended for its seafood. *Homestead Café*, at 21 Nordic Drive, offers good home cooking—the best in town, according to owner Diane. They are open 24 hours a day during the summer months. Closed Sunday. In the summertime, drinks and snacks are available at *Helse*, the natural food store, and there is also a pizza parlor and a Chinese take-out.

BRITISH COLUMBIA

We love traveling in Canada. Canadians in general are soft-spoken and cordial, and they are particularly friendly and helpful in the islands. Although Canada is so close and there is no language difficulty, a visit there provides the U.S. traveler with a welcome occasion to view the world from a different national perspective.

We have traveled to many islands around the world, but there is no more beautiful place to be than the Canadian islands during the long days of summer. The Canadian sunsets are unsurpassed, and the lingering, Maxfield Parrish-blue twilight, which lasts until almost eleven o'clock at night, is truly magical. Here, on these green, rocky islands, time seems to slow down. Talking with new and old friends long into the warm, still nights of summer is one of our favorite memories along the Pacific Coast.

It was Aideen Lydon of Victoria, B.C., who pointed out the difference between bed and breakfasts in Canada and the United States (of course, as soon as we generalize, someone will point out six examples to the contrary): B&Bs in Canada have kept closer to the British tradition of simply having a paying guest in the home, while in the United

States many B&Bs are really small inns.

We highly recommend Ms. Lydon's *Hibernia Bed and Breakfast*, 747 Helvetia Crescent, Victoria, B.C. V8Y 1M1, (604) 658-5519. It's located in a woodsy suburb near Elk Lake, fifteen minutes from the Sidney airport and only a little farther from the Sidney Harbour and Swartz Bay ferries. Aideen Lydon offers three rooms in her family home, which is full of mementos from Ireland and surrounded by a spacious garden. She genuinely enjoys what happens to people when they relax in her home. "People meet on the sun deck and talk for three hours," she says. "Sometimes they become lifelong friends. New Yorkers come here who haven't eaten breakfast for a year. They say, 'I'll just have something light.' Then they see what others are having and change their minds." What others are having is bacon, farm-fresh eggs, homemade breads, fruit, oatmeal, and good talk. Ms. Lydon is organist and choir director in a Victoria church, an avid reader, mother of five grown children, and a high-energy new friend. This is an ideal place from which to visit Victoria or set out on your quest for the perfect island.

Strait of Georgia Islands

Victoria, British Columbia, one of the loveliest small cities in the world, hosts thousands of visitors each year. Fewer vacationers have gone "up island" to explore the mountains, lakes, and coastline of Vancouver Island, and still fewer know the delights of the smaller islands that lie off the east coast of Vancouver in the Strait of Georgia. Of the many possibilities in the island group between Vancouver and the Canadian mainland, we've chosen four: Hornby, Denman, Quadra, and Cortes.

As it happens, the islands come in pairs; in each case, the outer island can be reached only by ferry from the one closer to shore. We went as far north as the town of Campbell River, renowned for its sportfishing, and took the ferry to Quadra and, crossing Quadra, to Cortes. In addition to having some rugged wilderness, Quadra is an angler's paradise; Cortes, although more remote, is somehow gentler. Denman, a little under 200 miles north of Victoria, and Hornby, reached by crossing Denman, are tamer, better known, and closer to Victoria than the other two. They are also smaller and more densely populated. Spectacular coastal scenery of islands, water, and mountains is combined in each case with the gentler landscape of beautiful farmland. These islands also boast a rich community and artistic life and a strong commitment to preserving the environment.

Because of their sheltered position and the Japanese current, the water temperature during the summer can often reach the seventies, which makes for ideal swimming, something almost impossible to do in the frosty waters of the Gulf and San Juan islands. These islands are also blessed with long, wide beaches, often fifty yards wide at low tide, an invitation to great walking.

People who have lived in Victoria all their lives may recognize the names Denman and Hornby, but Quadra and

LINDA LANCIONE MOYER

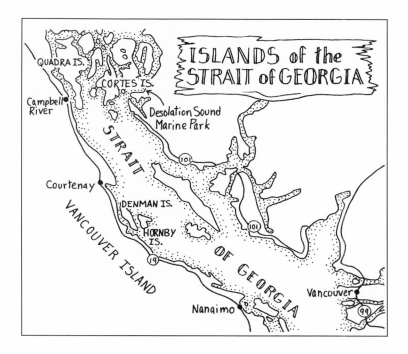

Cortes are likely to draw a blank. We found them to be ideal either for a brief offbeat excursion or a week or two of complete relaxation.

As you head north from Victoria, the first section of the highway is strikingly beautiful, with watery views in between the conifers, then stretches of open farm country. An interesting place to stop for coffee or lunch and a few photographs is Chemainus, a small town that a few years back was an almost bankrupt logging community. It turned itself around economically by painting charming historical murals on many of its buildings, drawing attention and business to the town.

Farther north, toward Ladysmith, the highway grows dense with roadside commercial eyesores: gas stations and fast food restaurants. (A two-car train leaves Victoria every morning at 8:00 for Courtenay, bypassing all the commercial activity.) This whole coastline is vacationland, with plenty of campgrounds, fishing, and boating. The two-lane highway is quite heavily traveled in the summer. But don't despair, soon you will be on the ferry and away from all that. It's amazing how even the briefest trip across the water can bring detachment and rest.

Hornby

Two of our favorite islands in British Columbia are Denman and Hornby, situated side by side offshore about a third of the way up the east coast of Vancouver Island. Since you must cross Denman to get to the Hornby ferry, the two islands are often spoken of in the same breath, as if they were Siamese twins linked by the umbilical cord of the ferry lines, but these two utterly special islands are quite different both in character and topography.

On Hornby, you leave the ferry landing and drive up the hill along Central Road, past lovely flat farmland that in spring glows green and gold in contrast to the austere, snowy mountains across the straits in the distance. You will pass the log-constructed community center, where locals and visitors meet for dances and movies, and soon arrive at the Hornby Coop, where all investigation of the island must begin. The Coop is a well-run, well-stocked, fairly priced general store we heard about long before we arrived

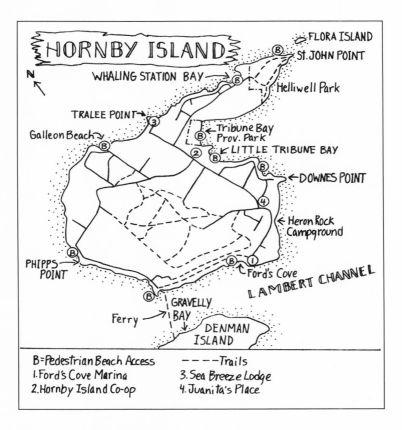

HORNBY ISLAND

FLORA ISLAND
St. JOHN POINT
WHALING STATION BAY →
Helliwell Park
N
TRALEE POINT →
Galleon Beach →
← Tribune Bay Prov. Park
LITTLE TRIBUNE BAY
← DOWNES POINT
← Heron Rock Campground
PHIPPS POINT →
Ford's Cove
LAMBERT CHANNEL
Ferry →
GRAVELLY BAY
DENMAN ISLAND

B = Pedestrian Beach Access   - - - - Trails
1. Ford's Cove Marina   3. Sea Breeze Lodge
2. Hornby Island Co-op   4. Juanita's Place

there which also serves as a village square gathering place
and locus for the entire island. On the broad front porch,
people congregate around the notice board and the public
telephone. Next to the store is a cluster of tiny shops known
as the ringside markets, which sell locally made crafts and
clothing and food in the summer.

Inside the Coop, the produce is fresh and the personnel very friendly. Beautiful postcards of the island are for

LINDA LANCIONE MOYER

sale, and you can buy stamps for them at the post office, which is housed in a walled-off corner of the building to the left as you enter the door. At the customer service counter behind the post office, you can cash a check or obtain a fishing license or a building permit. Downstairs you can find everything else you might need, such as hardware, outdoor furniture, or camping gear. In a loft overlooking the store (the stairs are toward the back) is Karen's Club Mezz, where we had coffee (they have an espresso machine) and home-baked treats and eavesdropped on the locals discussing the ferry schedule and who got a building permit for what. From this aerie, you look down on the sunlight glowing from the skylights above onto the bright

LINDA LANCIONE MOYER

yellow light fixtures, the red aproned checkers, the stacks of baskets for sale, and the bright, fresh produce. It's like looking at a Richard Scarry children's book version of the perfect small town store.

From the Coop, roads branch out to our three favorite spots on the island. A left turn off Central Road puts you on St. John Road. Go about 100 yards to the entrance to Tribune Bay Provincial Park on the right. The vast, protected bay is a perfect spot for swimmers, giving this part of the island its reputation as "little Hawaii." Edging the bay is a driftwood-strewn beach with a tennis court at the far end. There is a pleasant grassy area with picnic tables, but there is no camping.

If you do nothing else on Hornby, go to Helliwell Provincial Park. This is not just a park; it embraces some of the most splendid scenery in Canada. In fact, its six-mile hike ranks right up there among our ten best hikes ever. It arches around St. John Point, at the very tip of the peninsula that extends off the eastern end of the island, and thus affords views across the water in all directions.

To get there, continue down St. John Road and follow the signs to Whaling Station Bay. When the road forks toward the end, go to the right, past a small sign obscured by trees which indicates the park. (Sometimes we think Canadians are trying to keep their lovely provincial parks a secret.) About one-half mile up the road is the parking lot and the beginning of the loop. When the trail divides, go *left*, where a gentle walk leads through a forest of Douglas fir to the coast and gravelly, tide pool-rich coves backed by grassy, low-cropped headlands. The fine April morning we were there found a couple crouched over a tide pool examining its life, a mother sunning herself on a blanket as she read to her young son in German, and a solitary man in a watch cap sitting on a rock looking out to sea. We paused here on the sturdy bench overlooking the water to once again contemplate the lacy white mountains.

Continue to your right around the point where the cliffs begin to drop off steeply but the walk along the edge of the bluffs remains gentle. If the terrible grandeur of the expansive views wears on you, you can focus for a while on the waterfowl or sea mammals bobbing in the waters below or search for a glimpse of a bald eagle in the forests at your back. Here we laid down in a bed of yellow wildflowers, here we ate an apple, here we wrote in our notebook, "People are often disappointing, but nature never is."

LINDA LANCIONE MOYER

And then we got lost! Following the narrow path that edges the water and slopes upward, we ended up on private property—but with signs marking "trail" and "alternate." Following "alternate," a gravel road, we came out on St. John Road a couple of miles below the trailhead. So don't do that! Instead, cut uphill after the third bench *or* forgo the loop and turn around and retrace your steps. The first part is the best anyway. The loop is six kilometers and supposedly takes 1½ hours, but the sights are so splendid you will want to linger. There are pit toilets near the trailhead but no water in the park.

Our third favorite spot on the island is the campground at Heron Rocks, on the west side of the island, overlooking Lambert Channel between Denman and Hornby. Here, two ferries away from Vancouver Island, we felt like we'd found the end of the world, and it was splendid. Imagine a meadow backed by old growth forest, next to the sea. Imagine looking across the water at long, low Denman and the tiny lighthouse island at its tip, Chrome Island, and west of Denman, very near, the snowy mountains of Vancouver Island. Imagine a child—a large child—at play with driftwood, building makeshift shelters with walls and shelves and whimsical driftwood chairs facing out over the water. Imagine spring, with tiny purple grape hyacinths pushing up everywhere in the green grass and the leaves of the gnarled old oaks just unfurling. Imagine island light, doubled because given a second chance by the water. Imagine a magnificent orchestra made up of crows, gulls, woodpeckers, robins, and other songbirds playing morning and night. This shimmering location makes "primitive" camping worth the effort.

Idyllic Hornby, so close to the busy vacation territory of this part of Vancouver Island, is experiencing a certain amount of pressure for growth. Hornby is an island where lifelong islanders, architects and potters who have left the city in search of a more bucolic life, newly arrived retired couples, and Deadheads living in old school buses must work together to create a way of life that protects the place that they love and have chosen. So far, it seems to be working. Hilary Brown directs the Heron Rocks Friendship Centre, a small retreat and conference center for environmental and social change issues. A sturdy, thoughtful woman who has been on the island fifty-three years, she summed up the growth problem succinctly. "I don't mind

LINDA LANCIONE MOYER

people," she said, "but they expect more water, later ferries. They've got to understand that this is a rural community and not bring city standards here."

HOW TO GET THERE

Take the ferry to Denman from Buckley Bay, a wide spot in the road between Courtenay and Parksville, just above Fanny Bay. Buckley Bay is too small to be on any map, but the ferry is clearly indicated by signs along the highway. Cross Denman, a beautiful 13-minute drive through gorgeous farm country, on the clearly marked road to the Hornby ferry landing at Gravelly Bay. Arrival and departure of the two ferries are coordinated so you won't have to wait long. Each ferry crossing takes about ten minutes. Ferries leave almost hourly from Buckley Bay to Denman until 11:00 p.m., but the last ferry to Hornby is at 6:35 p.m. except on Friday. Check the ferry schedule for updates. Round-trip tickets for both ferries are purchased at Buckley Bay. Fare: $15.50.

WHERE TO STAY

Heron Rock is a spectacular place to camp. At the end of the road is *Ford's Marina*, a boating outpost with a tiny store, a campground, and several cabins. The most popular spot to camp is at *Tribune Bay*.

One way to solve the dilemma of where to eat on this island is to stay at *Sea Breeze Lodge*, Hornby, B.C. V0R 1T0, (604) 335-2321. There are eleven pleasant cottages on the beach, some with kitchens and fireplaces. Meals are served in the main house. It's open all year, but no meals are served off-season.

Juanita's Place, Arthur Road, R.R. 1, Hornby, B.C. V0R 1T0, (604) 335-0506. This is the only bed and breakfast we found that's open all year. Juanita, a grandmother who moved from eastern Canada only 2½ years ago "to be within spoiling distance of her granddaughter," offers two bedrooms, one with double beds, one with single, half a mile from a pleasant beach.

WHERE TO EAT

Upstairs in the Coop, the *Café Mezz* is open for breakfast and lunch. There used to be a café at the boat dock, but it burned down. A new one should be opening soon. In April, we found nowhere to eat dinner out on the island. This may be a plus if you're prepared to cope, as it surely is a factor in limiting tourist growth. The *Coop* has an abundance of good food you can prepare yourself.

There is a pleasant café at the ferry landing at Buckley Bay, before you leave Vancouver Island.

Denman

When we took the ferry back to Denman after exploring the wonders of Hornby, it seemed quite tame at first. It has a softer landscape than Hornby. The rolling, open farmland is very appealing and restful, and there are some stunning farmhouses overlooking pastureland and the water. Hornby is more wildly beautiful and, because of the two ferries, seems more removed from "civilization," yet at the same time more of a vacation destination than its neighbor. Denman Island is not a place that courts visitors. It's described

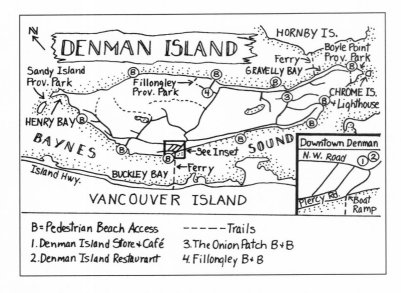

by a local resident as "more political than Hornby, with many people involved in the environmental movement, feminism, and the men's movement." It's also a haven for artists and gardeners. Signs for crafts studios abound.

The focal point of "Downtown Denman" is the Denman Island Store and Café, a creaky old general store with a limited selection of goods and adjoining café, which does a booming business since it's the only game in town. Up the road a new building was under construction; no one seemed quite sure if it would be a restaurant, a deli, or a hardware store. At the other end of town, just up from the ferry landing, stands a lovely old white wooden church.

There are three provincial parks on Denman, but only one is accessible by car. The other two are situated at either tip of the island. To get to Boyle Point Provincial Park, on the southeast tip, follow East Road to the Hornsby ferry landing, but instead of dropping to your left when the paved road ends, continue straight ahead on the unpaved road until it ends in about one mile. There are absolutely no signs to indicate the park's existence. Since it is a newly created park, perhaps there will be a sign by the time you get there. The way to the island's tip is indicated by a terse marker, "Lighthouse, 1 km." Follow the fire road on foot out to the point where there are two great viewing spots. From atop the sheer cliffs, you can look down on Chrome Island and its lighthouse, a broad expanse of water in all directions which has for its background the mountains. This is a great place to sketch or take photographs or simply bring a picnic to eat among the madrone (arbutus, in Canada), firs, and rhododendrons as you watch the seals frolic in the placid waters below and listen to their constant chatter.

Fillongley State Park, located slightly north of the eastern end of the main road across the island, encompasses a stretch of beach as well as some lovely trails through the woods.

At the northwest end of the island is Sandy Island Marine Park, where there are picnic areas and long stretches of sandy beach. At low tide you can walk out to Sandy Island, a nesting place for bald eagles, but make sure you time it so that you can get back. Or rent a canoe and paddle out there.

HOW TO GET THERE

Take the ferry from Buckley Bay (see Hornby).

LINDA LANCIONE MOYER

WHERE TO STAY

Fillongley Bed and Breakfast, 1795 Swan Road, Denman, B.C. V0R 1T0, (604) 335-2625. This inviting place is situated on hilly farmland just across from the entrance to Fillongley Park. Collin Barrow, the British proprietor, designed his house himself and participated in its construction. It has a large, welcoming combination kitchen and living room and three bedrooms available to guests, one with three single beds for friends traveling together. Barrow, as he modestly puts it, "likes to grow things"; he has grafted English varieties of apples onto the varieties he found in British Columbia. Mr. Barrow had just opened his home to guests when we arrived on Denman. On the strength of the hospitality we received there, we would highly recommend it as a place to stay. Inexpensive.

The Onion Patch Bed and Breakfast, 9151 Keith Wagner Way, Denman, B.C. V0R 1T0, (604) 335-2014. Clive and Heather Openshaw's modern wood house has three upstairs rooms, two doubles and a single, reached by a spiral staircase. In the morning, guests are treated to a fresh fruit plate, omelets, and home-baked scones. Here you can make yourself at home in the spacious living room or enjoy the bucolic, tree-ringed surroundings, including the pigs and sheep the owners keep. A jeweler by trade, Clive works in precious metals and also sets stones; he likes to have guests visit his workshop on the premises. He says returning visitors get into the habit of bringing their jewelry for repairs. The Openshaws stay open all year, and Clive points out that the ski resorts of the Comox Valley on Vancouver Island are only an hour away.

Balla Machree, 2650 Jemima, Denman Island, B.C.

LINDA LANCIONE MOYER

V0R 1T0, (604) 335-2541. *Balla Machree* means "home of my heart" in Gaelic, ex-logger Rick Harris tells us. He and his Irish wife have two bedrooms to offer guests. The upstairs room has a skylight and vaulted ceilings as does the upstairs bath, which boasts a two-person soaker tub and two-person shower. The plainer room downstairs has both a queen and a single bed. The house is situated at the end of an 800-foot lane on ten acres of cedar forest. The Harrises present a full country breakfast, including eggs from their own range-fed chickens, and Ro Harris says that if pressed, she'll even serve up a high-cholesterol Ulster fry. Since the house is full of antiques, it's not suitable for young children, but children over twelve are welcome. For a nominal extra charge, you can also arrange to go out on Rick's fishing boat with him.

Fillongley Provincial Park has campsites for RVs on the beach.

WHERE TO EAT

Denman Café, located in the Denman Island Store, was the only option when we were there in April. They serve soups, sandwiches, salads, a few entrées, breakfasts, and delicious-looking desserts at a few tables indoors and on their sunny terrace. In summer, dinner is served at the *Denman Island Guest House and Restaurant*.

For further information about Denman and Hornby, contact Denman/Hornby Tourist Services, Denman, B.C. V0R 1T0, (604) 335-2293.

Quadra

When the ferry docks at Quathiaski Cove, you think you know immediately what kind of place you're in from the bristly looking salmon boats standing cheek by jowl in the harbor. This is a place where men sit around in the tavern late in the afternoon talking about loran readings and thirty-pound salmon catches. But that's not all. As we drive inland, a mailbox dressed in a rainbow of colors proclaims "TAROT READINGS." So alongside the fishing the island is known for, there must be bits of counterculture hidden in the woods.

"Wild," "bleak," "imposing," "rugged" are some of the adjectives we heard applied to Quadra. There are hikes to take and beaches to comb on this island, but the main reason people come here is to fish. Quadra is across the channel from Campbell River, a major location for sport-fishing. Campbell River is overbuilt, crowded, and crammed with motels and restaurants. The island offers the same fishing opportunities but without the hype and bustle. The big resorts all include fishing in their advertising. This is a sportsman's world, but even if you don't fish, it would make a good getaway for a vacation or a weekend of hiking, kayaking, diving, or whale- or bird-watching. There are many lakes to explore; canoes can be rented at Heriot Bay. There are nine well-maintained hiking trails ranging from forty-minute strolls to four- or five-hour climbs.

Quadra is a nature lover's paradise. Its waters are clear and rich with sea life, including harbor seals, sea lions, and, seasonally, pods of killer whales. Cormorants, grebes, ducks, scoters, and mergansers winter here, and the snowy owl and peregrine falcon, along with wolves and cougars, have been spotted at the north end of the island. Other animals in the abundant forests include black-tailed deer, raccoons, and river otters.

In the nineteenth century, long before the growth of Campbell River, Quadra was a center of logging and mining. A fishing cannery was established in 1904. Quathiaski Cove, where the ferry from Vancouver Island docks, was a busy community in those days, and it's still the principal settlement on the island. Pick up your provisions here at Quadra Foods and stop at the local pub, called the Landing. About fifteen minutes due north on the narrow southern

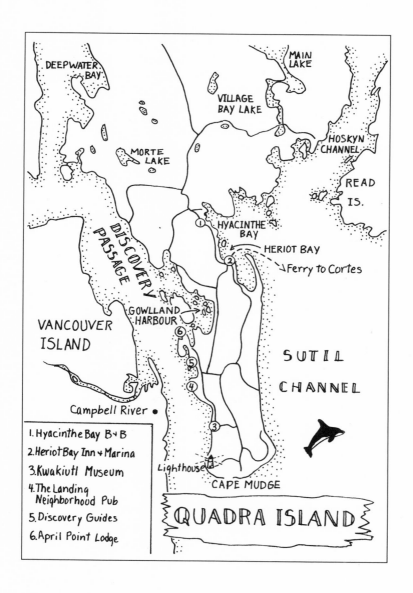

DEEPWATER BAY

MAIN LAKE

VILLAGE BAY LAKE

HOSKYN CHANNEL

MORTE LAKE

READ IS.

DISCOVERY PASSAGE

HYACINTHE BAY

HERIOT BAY

Ferry to Cortes

VANCOUVER ISLAND

GOWLLAND HARBOUR

SUTIL

CHANNEL

Campbell River •

1. Hyacinthe Bay B + B
2. Heriot Bay Inn + Marina
3. Kwakiutl Museum
4. The Landing Neighborhood Pub
5. Discovery Guides
6. April Point Lodge

Lighthouse

CAPE MUDGE

QUADRA ISLAND

section of the island is Heriot Bay, the other major (but not large) locus of activity, dominated by Heriot Bay Inn, which has a pub and restaurant. The inn, built in 1984 and twice restored after fires, fronts the water and has its own marina. The ferry to Cortes leaves from Heriot Bay.

Of the roughly 200 sportfishing resorts along the British Columbia coast, the newly opened Tsa-Kwa-Luten Lodge on the southern tip of the island at Cape Mudge is unique. Owned and operated by the Cape Mudge band of the Kwagiutl Nation, it combines sportfishing with a native cultural experience. The 4,000-square-foot main lodge is a re-creation of a native longhouse. Pam Holloway, cultural events coordinator, promises a full schedule of events that include traditional dances, island singers, and wares created by native artists. Traditional dance ceremonies take place between dinner seatings in the dining room twice a week.

Pam Holloway, herself a member of the Kwagiutl Nation, wishes to present an enlightening cultural experience to the public without in any way demeaning or trivializing the native traditions, which are religious in nature. She is careful to talk about regalia rather than costume, ceremony rather than performance. The word *tsa-kwa-luten* means "gathering place" in the Kwakwala language; she sees the lodge as an extension of her people's tradition of hospitality.

The thriving native community at Cape Mudge is made up of fishing people: like others on the island, they operate commercial seine boats for salmon and herring. Ms. Holloway attributes the long-standing self-sufficiency and prosperity of her community to former Chief Bill Assu's commitment to education for his people and co-

LINDA LANCIONE MOYER

operation with the nonnative people in the logging and fishing industries early in the century.

One of the triumphs of this community is the Kwagiutl Museum, opened in 1979. Its potlatch collection features sacred ceremonial objects and cedar bark regalia that were used in Kwagiutl Winter Ceremonies. The masks, head-dresses, coppers, and other objects were confiscated by the federal government in 1922, when a law banning the Pot-latch was enforced. Kwagiutl leaders were forced to sur-render their regalia or face a prison sentence. The National Museum agreed in the late 1970s to return the artifacts on condition that a state-of-the-art museum was available to house them. Thus this museum, with its attractive, semi-circular walls, was born.

The museum also features a selection of photographs of Kwagiutl villages from the turn of the century and a gift shop with contemporary Kwagiutl art objects and books about Kwagiutl culture and local natural history. It is open Tuesday through Saturday, 1:00 to 4:30 p.m. year-round. Extended summertime hours are: June, Tuesday through Saturday, 10:00 a.m. to 4:30 p.m.; July and August, Monday through Saturday, 10:00 a.m. to 7:30 p.m.; Sunday, noon to 4:30 p.m.

Cape Mudge is also where Captain Vancouver first set foot on the island.

HOW TO GET THERE

Drive to Campbell River, about halfway up Vancouver Island on the east side, and take the ferry from there. The ferry makes many crossings a day, until late in the evening. The ride is 12 to 15 minutes and costs $6.00 Canadian. Air Canada and Canadian Airlines International also fly daily to Campbell River, with connections in Vancouver and Seattle.

WHERE TO STAY

Heriot Bay Inn and Marina, P.O. Box 100, Heriot Bay, B.C. V0P 1H0, (604) 285-3322. This handsome old blue and white resort on the waterfront overlooking Heriot Bay offers a bed-and-breakfast arrangement in the inn as well as cottages with kitchens and fireplaces, RV hookups, and boat moorage. Moderate.

April Point Lodge, P.O. Box 1, Campbell River, B.C. V9W 4Z9, (604) 285-2222. Located on April Point near

Quathiaski Cove, this lodge has been family owned and operated for forty years. It offers cabins and rooms from April 15 to October 15. The lodge, primarily oriented to a fishing clientele, has its own boats and a staff of guides. Conferences are held there outside of fishing season.

Tsa-Kwa-Luten Lodge, P.O. Box 460, Quathiaski Cove, B.C. V0P 1N0, (604) 285-2042 or 1-800-665-7745 (reservations). Expensive.

Hyacinthe Bay Bed and Breakfast, P.O. Box 343, Heriot Bay, Quadra Isle, B.C. V0P 1H0, (604) 285-2126. At the north end of Heriot Bay, this B&B is located along a woodsy residential street with a view of the water through trees. The owner writes cookbooks, so breakfast here is a real treat, and dinner can sometimes be arranged as well. They offer a sun deck with hot tub and a private bath. Inexpensive.

Joha House, Quathiaski Cove, B.C. V0P 1N0, (604) 285-2247. If you want a B&B that's near the ferry or the boat harbor at Quathiaski Cove, this is for you. Joyce and Harold Johnson (thus, Joha) bought their modern glass and wood house six or seven years ago and have done a lot of work to make it lovely. They offer two traditional bed and breakfast rooms with a shared bath, as well as a garden suite with a private entrance (3-night minimum) and a beach cottage (one-week minimum). They even offer guest moorage at their own dock. Inexpensive/moderate.

WHERE TO EAT

Heriot Bay Inn has a full restaurant in season. Their smoky, friendly pub is open all year and serves reasonably priced lunches. The clam chowder is especially tasty.

Across the island at Quathiaski Cove is another atmospheric pub, *The Landing*. *April Point Lodge* serves three meals a day when open and requests reservations. In season, there's also *Beaver's Family Restaurant* in Heriot Bay where you can take out a pizza or eat in. *Tsa-Kwa-Luten Lodge* at Cape Mudge has a large dining room. It's expensive.

Cortes

Cortes Island was named in 1792 for Spanish explorer Hernando Cortés, conqueror of Mexico, by officers Galiano and Valdes of the Spanish navy, whose names are borne by other islands in the region. The name Sutil, which means "subtle" in Spanish and is found throughout the region, was the name of one of their schooners,

Cortes, 40 minutes from Quadra by ferry, covers 116 square miles. Although described as a gentle island, after Denman and Hornby, Cortes struck us as sprawling, sparsely populated, and very wooded. All the roads are on the southern half of the island; in the north are fish farms, a tree farm, and boat anchorages.

From the ferry landing, the road fishhooks around to Whaletown, a former whaling station and now a tiny outpost with a minuscule post office and a general store run by a pleasant British woman. There's a pretty little rock garden in front of the store overlooking the bay. Coming out of Whaletown, follow the Whaletown Road to Robertson Road, where a right turn will bring you to red-painted

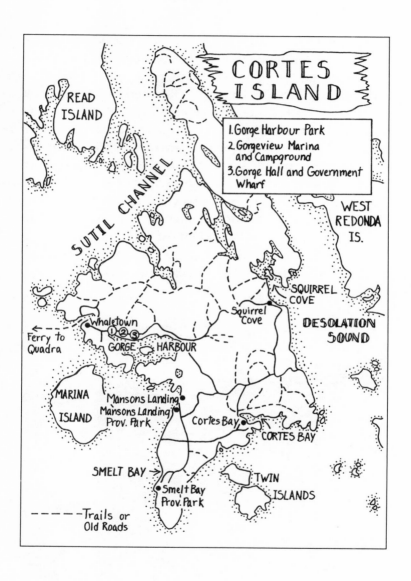

CORTES ISLAND

1. Gorge Harbour Park
2. Gorgeview Marina and Campground
3. Gorge Hall and Government Wharf

READ ISLAND

SUTIL CHANNEL

WEST REDONDA IS.

SQUIRREL COVE

Squirrel Cove

DESOLATION SOUND

Ferry to Quadra

Whaletown
①②③
GORGE HARBOUR

MARINA ISLAND

Mansons Landing
Mansons Landing Prov. Park

Cortes Bay

CORTES BAY

SMELT BAY →

Smelt Bay Prov. Park

TWIN ISLANDS

- - - - Trails or Old Roads

Government Wharf on Gorge Harbour, a beautiful bay comparable in shape to San Francisco Bay with only a tiny narrow gorge giving onto the larger waters.

Here we met local residents Ron and Helen applying paint to the hull of their beautiful sailboat. Ron is a movie grip who works in Vancouver. His union calls him on the island when they have a job for him; meanwhile, he enjoys life in the country and on the water. Like Ron, many of the residents of the Northwest islands whom we met go off island to work for part of the week or the year.

From Gorge Harbour, Whaletown Road meanders across the island. Making a right on Sutil Point Road, we drove past Sunflint Lake, Hague Lake, and Manson's Landing, continuing south until we reached Smelt Bay Provin-

LINDA LANCIONE MOYER

cial Park, again almost missing it because there was no sign. At the end of Sutil Point Road, take the right road of the three-pronged fork. Here there is excellent camping in wooded sites and an easy walk down to Smelt Bay.

Arriving at Smelt Bay on an April evening, we felt like the first explorers must have. We leaned against a huge driftwood log and listened to the water lap the shore as the crisscrossing paths of the waterbirds cast shadows over the water. At our backs, two horses grazed unfenced. Then we began to notice the handsome homes along the wooded shoreline. Soon three young people on horseback cantered along the beach and joggers appeared. Clearly, a fortunate few have already staked their claim.

Going north on Sutil Point Road, take a right on Bartholemew Road and drive to Cortes Bay, where there are some lovely beaches and walks. Then you can continue north to Squirrel Cove, where there is an Indian village. The island was Salish Indian territory until they were killed by the smallpox epidemic of 1862. The Indians at Squirrel Cove today are Klahuse Salish who settled on Cortes in the 1890s.

This side of the island faces onto Desolation Sound and is an area rich with animal and bird life.

For all its quiet, empty appearance, much goes on here. Cortes is home to Hollyhock Farm, a center that offers workshops and private and group retreats, and Linnea Farms, run in cooperation with Turtle Island, a land preservation group. Oyster cultivation is important here, and oysters and clams are available for the taking along the beach. Apparently beer making is a thriving cottage industry on the island. At Taka Mika, you can buy a local beer on tap.

Modern services from the mainland were late in coming to the island. A regular ferry service began in 1969, and electricity dates only from 1970.

Local residents express the usual ambivalence toward any influx of visitors. "At least tourism is a nonpolluting industry," says Paul, a social worker from the United States who has lived on the island for twenty years. Many of the islanders are environmentalists who have managed to put a stop to clear-cutting on the island, although some logging is still done. "People are starting to realize that there is great tourism potential up here," says Paul, "and that they shouldn't cut down what tourists come to see."

Cortes is lovely, quiet, and removed. Little by little, the resident population increases and so does the number of visitors. But Cortes doesn't put on make-up and get all tarted up for the guests. It stays its lovely, natural self.

HOW TO GET THERE

Take the ferry from Campbell River to Quadra. Then it's a ten-minute drive to Heriot Bay for the ferry to Cortes.

WHERE TO STAY

Highly recommended by local residents is *Fairhaven Farm Bed and Breakfast*, Box 141, Manson's Landing, Cortes Island, B.C. V0P 1K0, (604) 935-6501. David and Margaret Hansen offer two rooms in their log and frame house, one with shared bath. Breakfast, including brown eggs from their farm and homemade breads and jams, can be served outside under the grape arbor. Lunch and dinner will also be prepared on request. Fairhaven Farms is near the beach and Cortes Bay. Inexpensive.

LINDA LANCIONE MOYER

In a similar location is *Victoria Summers Bed and Breakfast*, Box 6, Manson's Landing, Cortes Island, B.C. V0P 1K0, (604) 935-6594, which offers a single or double with shared bath and a breakfast that includes homemade bread and jam. Victoria Summers notes that her place is only a two-minute walk from the Taka Mika restaurant and the newly opened Cortes Market and a fifteen-minute walk from Sandy Beach. Children and smokers are welcome, but pets are not. Inexpensive.

Wolf Bluff Castle Bed and Breakfast, Manzanita Road, Cortes Bay, Cortes Island, B.C. V0P 1K0, (604) 935-6764. Here is host Karl Triller's description: "Chef-cook, baker, homesteader, woodcarver. Rustic and antique, 1990 owner-built castle with three towers and all amenities, in wooded setting. Hiking trails to unsurpassed views of Desolation Sound." He doesn't mention the bas-reliefs on the interior walls, the huge collection of hand-tied fishing flies, and the outdoor sanitary facilities. Definitely an eccentric, one-man operation. Inexpensive.

Blue Heron Bed and Breakfast, Box 23, Manson's Landing, Cortes Island, B.C. V0P 1K0, (604) 935-6584. Emilia and Gunnar Hansen recently began to offer two lovely rooms, one with private bath, in a garden setting with views overlooking Sutil Bay and a nearby beach.

WHERE TO EAT

At one point, hungry, we found ourselves wondering why someone doesn't start a really fine restaurant here, a French family, maybe, who could do justice to local salmon, oysters, clams, and venison. However, that's not the nature of the place. Instead, there is *Taka Mika* at Manson's Landing,

BURL WILLES

which has a pretty standard menu, an attractive terrace, and a salad bar and is fully licensed. Across the street from Taka Mika is the *Cortes Community Center,* where, on the days the post office is open, a coffee shop in the building serves breakfast and lunch. *Gorge Harbour Marina* has a restaurant that is open only in summer.

Gulf Islands

Each of the Gulf Islands has its special characteristics. Mayne has the oldest buildings and the richest history, Galiano is the most "arty," North and South Pender are the closest to the United States. The most distant, Saturna, is the quietest, the least populated and the least visited. They have in common a special beauty and serenity that continues to draw people to them. After spending several years sailing around the world, painter Evan Berghan and his Sri Lankan/Malaysian wife, Christina, have chosen to make Mayne their permanent home. Evan says, "I wanted a quiet island of pine, rocks, and coves, where one is inspired to paint at every turn of coastline. In all our travels, only the Ryukyu islands of Southern Japan can compare with the beauty of the Gulf Islands."

Mayne

Mayne, the smallest of the southern Gulf Islands, lies between Galiano, Pender, and Saturna. The mainland of Vancouver is clearly visible from the beach at Oyster Bay or the peak of Mount Parke. The closest to the mainland, Mayne

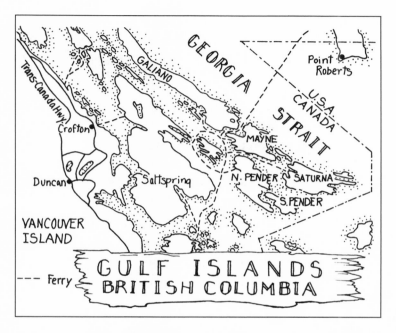

is also the most densely populated for its size. Its five by three miles support 700 permanent residents, a population that doubles during the summer. The impact of the residents on the island seems light, since they are all here to get away from it all and enjoy the unpolluted environment. Visitors come by ferry during the summer either to hike or cycle the island. Some hope to buy summer homes here, and there are enough real estate agents to keep them busy. It's a great low-cost vacation spot for families.

Local businesses thrive during the tourist season. Miners Bay, the "downtown" of Mayne, is where most of the eight stores are. Getting from Village Bay ferry terminal to Miners Bay is an easy enough task, as there is only one main road around the island. The post office, established in 1880, doubles as an information center, thanks to Betty, the knowledgeable postmistress. This is a good source of reading material as well: back issues of *Time* and *National Geographic* and old paperbacks lie for the taking under the bulletin board. Betty will be retiring soon, and the future of the post office is uncertain. But one thing *is* certain: Mayne islanders won't let this 111-year-old institution die without a fight.

Farther up the road are the grocery stores. The Mayne Open Market sells the most luscious organic produce in the

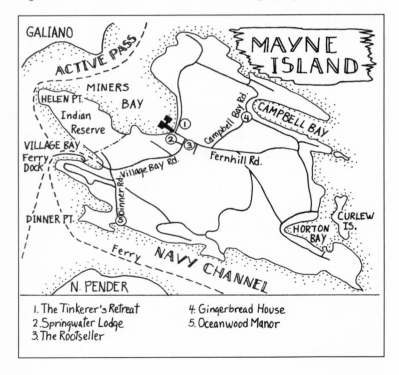

1. The Tinkerer's Retreat
2. Springwater Lodge
3. The Rootseller
4. Gingerbread House
5. Oceanwood Manor

Northwest. Most of it is locally grown. Rosalind, who sometimes works behind the cash register, treats customers to some of her homemade items such as salsa, hummus, tzatziki, and sorbets, all guaranteed to make the taste buds tingle. Here you'll also find herbs and local eggs. Milk products are still sold in recyclable glass bottles. Owner Ron Pither keeps a varied schedule, running between farms and also finding time to do community work at home as well as in Ometepe, Nicaragua, a sister island to the Gulf Islands. Next to the market you'll find fresh-baked croissants, breads, and pastries at Manna Bakery. Christina, the proprietor, runs a bustling café that in summer serves as a meeting ground for people from all over the United States and Canada to gather for coffee and pastry as they begin their day.

A two-minute walk to the Miners Bay dock reveals a dilapidated old building known as Springwater Lodge. The "deputy," a young man whose self-appointed title derives from his constant walks through the islands, pointed out the incredible view from here. The lodge overlooks the Active Pass channel, plied by ferries and ships. According to the locals, it is the most active passage in British Columbia. The lodge was built in the 1890s when miners used it as a stopover between Vancouver Island and the mainland during the time of dories and steam vessels that preceded the railroads. Today the funky, wood-paneled lodge, with its uneven floors, operates as a budget-priced hotel. The restaurant boasts a varied menu of fresh local garden and sea produce. We'll never forget the spectacular Canadian sunset as we dined al fresco at the lodge in early September, lingering over dessert in the twilight.

BURL WILLES

Behind the lodge, Sigrid Goobie, better known as the pickle lady, displays and sells her wares to the public during the summer. Other craftspeople set up tents nearby, giving the whole town a "fair" atmosphere. The local weekly paper helps the visitor track down local craftspeople and is also a good source for sports information (trail rides, sailing, fishing charters), B&Bs, and cabin and house rentals.

Of particular interest is the Wild Thyme Herb Farm. A one-hour walk or shorter bike ride from the ferry terminal brings you to Tinkler Road, where a green and yellow sign announces the farm. You will be welcomed by Russell, the farm dog, and Ann Johnson, the proprietor of this garden of the senses, which includes medicinal and cooking herbs, pesticide herbs, and herbal teas. Ann will be happy to show you around. Her fresh cut herbs, flowers, and vinegars make ideal gifts.

The history of the island goes back 6,000 years to the first aboriginal settlements, fed by the bounty of Active Pass. Sometime in the 1800s gold miners started docking here, and some began to settle, raising sheep and establishing orchards. During the next century agriculture expanded, mostly for export to the mainland. Japanese fishermen were here before World War II; several of them preferred to grow produce on dry land. Today the most abundant vegetable garden (with shoulder-high corn) belongs to a long-time Japanese resident. Now most of the agriculture feeds only the locals and those on surrounding islands.

Walking around the island is the way to discover the secret industries of the local community. For example, a couple cycled by on an ancient bicycle, none of your super-high-tech stuff. Stopping for a chat, they told us that the island is full of wildflower species. Mr. Simpson, who photographs and writes articles for the local *Island Tides* newspaper, never fails to discover a new species. His wife, Ann, weaves clothes and wall hangings from local sheep wool. Their studio is about two minutes from the ferry terminal. Known as Greenhouse Studio, it is open regularly during the summer and in the winter, by appointment.

Summer temperatures run around 30°C, but swimming takes some courage as the water temperatures do not exceed 20°C. The warmest waters are around David's Cove, about an hour walk from downtown Miners Bay. Campbell Bay is a jewel, but access is a little difficult, through brush and steep descents. There are a few paths made by the locals.

The island, which has not been intensively logged, has a subtropical feel because of the thick foliage and the majestically tall trees. Some of the oldest stands of trees are along Village Bay Road, which makes this road feel more like a country lane than a main thoroughfare. There is no hunting allowed on the island, so the wildlife population —including black-tail deer, harbor seals and sea lions, raccoons, otters, squirrels, and bald eagles—is fairly docile.

HOW TO GET THERE

Situated halfway between Vancouver and Victoria, Mayne Island is a short (approximately one hour) ferry ride, costing $4.00 round-trip from either Vancouver (Tsawwassen Terminal) or Victoria (Swartz Bay Terminal). Mayne is the transfer point for the Gulf Island ferry routes, and the frequent sailings (4-5 per day) to and from Mayne make it an ideal base for visiting other Gulf Islands. Vehicle reservations are recommended between the mainland and Mayne Island and on summer weekends from Swartz Bay. For 24-hour recorded schedule information, call B.C. Island Ferries at (604) 656-0757 in Victoria and (604) 685-1021 in Vancouver.

There is floatplane service ($49.00 each way) from Vancouver Harbour and from Vancouver Airport: Harbour Air, telephone (604) 688-1277.

WHERE TO STAY

Oceanwood Country Inn, C-2 Leighton Lane, R.R. 1, Mayne Island, B.C. V0N 2J0, (604) 539-5074, fax (604) 539-3002. Marilyn and Jonathan Chilvers bought this

Tudor-style house set on ten acres of forested land on an idyllic cove overlooking Navy Channel. They spared no expense to expand and restore it. When it opened in April 1990, it immediately became one of the most tasteful, comfortable, and luxurious small country inns in the Gulf Islands. Three of the rooms have their own fireplaces and whirlpool baths; two have private decks; three have large French doors opening onto the garden terrace. There is a living room, a library, and a game room and a dining room for breakfast and dinner. The Chilvers welcome dinner reservations from nonguests. Moderate to expensive.

Springwater Lodge, Miners Bay, Mayne Island, B.C. V0N 2J0, (604) 539-5521. Built on the oceanfront during the 1890s, Springwater is the oldest continuously operated hotel in British Columbia. Budget travelers happily overlook its noisy, well-worn, funky atmosphere. Inexpensive.

Gingerbread House, Campbell Bay Road, Mayne Island, B.C. V0N 2J0, (604) 539-3133. This is a lovingly restored Victorian home atop a small, nicely landscaped hill facing one of the most beautiful bays we've seen in Canada. On the far side of the bay, sculptured rock formations rise from the emerald green water. Above this long, continuous wall of convoluted stone grows a mass of magnificent conifers unbroken by any human-made structure. Moderate to expensive.

The *Tinkerer's Retreat*, Box 8, Mayne Island, B.C. V0N 2J0, (604) 539-2280. A few steps from Miners Bay and the village, the Tinkerer's Retreat is the most colorful and whimsical building on the island, surrounded by a wonderful garden of edible and medicinal herbs and flowering vines. This is an Elderhostel campus; upstairs is a small dor-

BURL WILLES

mitory for families or groups of people who are already friends. Rental bicycles are available. Owners Judith and Jurgen Englehardt are very enthusiastic about their off-season occupation, running a travel and language program. They especially enjoy having foreign visitors come to stay.

Blue Vista Resort, Bennett Bay, Mayne Island, B.C. V0N 2J0, (604) 539-2463. Blue Vista Resort's fully equipped cabins on tranquil Bennett Bay are especially popular with families during the summer. Each cabin has a fireplace, a kitchen, and a sun deck. Moderate.

Fernhill Lodge, Box 140, Mayne Island, B.C. V0N 2J0, (604) 539-2544. Hidden among the trees up a long private driveway, the all-wood Fernhill Lodge blends perfectly into its woodsy setting. Inside, there are seven suites, each with different decor: Jacobean, Colonial, Oriental, French, Edwardian. The most elaborate and certainly the most exotic on the island are the newly opened East Indian and Moroccan suites, each with a deck and hot tub. Each suite has a private entrance. The breakfast menu is two pages long, and dinners in the restaurant often have a historical theme: Renaissance, medieval, Roman. There is a sauna next to the herb garden. Expensive.

The Rootseller Bed and Breakfast, P.O Box 5, Village Bay Road, Mayne Island, B.C. V0N 2J0, (604) 539-2621. Mrs. Drummond, the friendly longtime owner of this cozy farmhouse in the heart of the village, welcomes cyclists and hikers. Inexpensive.

Island Tides, the local newspaper, lists other B&B establishments that we didn't have a chance to see. To obtain a copy, call (604) 539-5015 or fax (604) 539-2545. Reservations are required for all accommodations.

WHERE TO EAT

Springhill Lodge's waterfront deck is a local gathering spot for drinks and good food facing Miners Bay in the village. *Fernhill Lodge* is open to the public for dinner and Sunday brunch. Telephone 539-2544 for reservations. *Oceanwood Country Inn* welcomes nonresidents for dinner. There is a fireplace for chilly days and a solarium extension for sunny views of the garden. Extensive wine list. Reservations, telephone 539-5074. If you prefer a picnic, the local *deli* serves up wonderful sandwiches and hot pies to go.

Galiano

The trip by ferry from Mayne Island to Galiano Island takes 25 minutes. The island, fifteen miles long and about a mile wide, is in the shape of a club, with the handle turned northwest. The main road runs along the west ridge about 300 feet above sea level. Porlier Pass Road, the only road up the island, is about 17 miles long, straight but by no means tedious, with wonderful views of the water and neighboring islands.

About three-quarters of the island is owned by forestry giant Macmillan Bloedel. Residents now vote on the future purchase of forestry lands in order to retain the island's parklike state. Most stands of forests here are in their second or third growth. Logging would be devastating to the island and its economy, which depends on tourism.

Once on shore, we visited the local tourist information office to gather maps and brochures about accommodations and available sports activities, which include kayaking courses and rentals, diving, canoe and catamaran excursions, golf, fishing and bike rentals.

The Galiano Market, near the tourist information center, does not look unusual from the road. Inside, beyond the organic produce, a light airy room with a high ceiling has been lovingly built from polished local timber. This is Lony's Cozy Café, an island gathering spot. The slate fireplace is a work of art, as is everything on the walls or hanging from the ceiling. Sunlight poured through the skylight, and our wooden tables gleamed a golden yellow. We lingered long in this cozy spot, ordering more and more from

the kitchen's offerings of hearty soups, salads, freshly squeezed fruit drinks, and the special of the day, enchiladas.

Opposite this market is another grocery store, with an eye-catching craft store next to it. Its doorway is constructed of a couple of tree trunks blended into the building, and colorful hand-loomed bags from Guatemala hang under the eaves, reminiscent of a hut somewhere in South America. Ixchel, the name of the shop, means "Goddess of Medicine" in the Mayan culture. Heidi, who runs the store six days a week, explains that most of the crafts are done by women from all over the globe, including the Gulf Islands. By helping them to sell internationally, she assures that they get a fair price for their crafts. We were impressed with the quality of the items on sale and bought several locally made chenille scarves, a small rug, earrings, and a necklace.

Cottage industries dot the island. We found out about them from the tourist information office in Sturdies Bay, but they are sometimes listed in the local newspapers.

The scenic route around the island is via Montague Harbour to Porlier Pass Road. The harbor itself is a jewel, well protected by the substantial surrounding hills. It has been made into a provincial park, with campgrounds that are nearly always full in the summer. Other parks such as Bellhouse and Galiano Bluffs are equally attractive. Bell-house, a rocky peninsula that slopes gently to the sea at the northwest entrance of Active Pass, is accessible by car. From your picnic table here you can look out across the channel to Mayne Island, and on a clear day, the snowy peak of Mount Baker in Washington State is visible. This is a great fishing spot as the shoreline drops sharply to deep water and the tides are high. Galiano Bluffs is 300 feet or more above the pass, with views overlooking the pass and surrounding islands.

Local wildlife thrives on this island as three-quarters of it is wilderness. "Beware of Bears" signs are posted on all notice boards: the island had a run-in with a couple of bears that apparently landed there accidentally by way of floating logs. Land has been flooded by streams dammed by the local beaver brigade, the annoyance of flooding offset to some extent by the pleasures of the new freshwater pools they have created.

BURL WILLES

Galiano's early settlers grew vegetables and fruit, raised sheep, and supplemented their diet with fish and venison. Families like the Georgesons started cultivating their land in the 1800s. Most of the early settlers have been forgotten except for road signs bearing their names: Cook, MacClure, Ganner, Burril. The Japanese also played their part in the history of the island, working in the herring salteries on the shores of Active Pass. The native Indians of today live on reservations at the north end of the island, around Lighthouse Bay, but visitors should not disturb their privacy.

The early settlers lived in hand-hewn log homes. Many of the houses on the island today follow this tradition but with more light and space. One structure that is very impressive is Thymeways, a yoga and health enhancement retreat, which is Japanese country style in design. Local people, many active in its construction, say it has an energy of its own. It is the only yoga retreat in the southern Gulf Islands. The rock gardens that surround the house continue the Japanese tradition with bonsai and red maple. The view from the house of sea, stone, and pine is pure serenity. Even in Japan, we've rarely seen a finer marriage of site and structure. For further information about this special place, inquire at Thymeways, 790 Devina Drive, R.R. 2, Galiano Island, B.C. V0N 1P0, (604) 539-5071.

Buddhism has had an influence on the younger community here. A shrine at the northern end of the island, off Devina Drive near Coon Bay, was built by the Burmese Community of Vancouver. Its members make a yearly pilgrimage here which draws many local participants to the ceremonies. This is definitely not the norm for life in conservative Canada, but tolerance is a way of life in the islands, especially Galiano.

From the island's northern tip, the drive back to Sturdies Bay along the rocky coastline invites the visitor to linger. Idyllic coves with rocky, pine-clad islets, each one more enticing than the last, look very Japanese. The Spanish Hill Store and Café has an outdoor deck overlooking one of these coves. We basked in the warm sunlight with caffe lattes; the deep emerald water of the cove was mirror calm.

HOW TO GET THERE

Sturdies Bay is the ferry terminal for all British Columbia ferries. The ferry from Swartz Bay (Victoria) stops at Mayne before Sturdies. From Tsawwassen (Vancouver), the B.C. ferry stops 3 to 4 times daily en route to Swartz Bay via Mayne. For 24-hour recorded schedule information, call B.C. Island Ferries at (604) 656-0757 in Victoria and (604) 685-1021 in Vancouver.

Floatplane service is also available through Harbour Air, telephone (604) 688-1277.

WHERE TO STAY

Cliff Pagoda, Montague Harbour Road, Galiano, B.C. V0N 1P0, (604) 539-5436. Perched on a cliff overlooking Montague Harbour, this bed and breakfast is a small handcrafted three-level building in the shape of a Chinese pagoda. The top room, accessible by ladder, is a cozy eagle's nest with views to all sides. Friendly raccoons often outnumber the guests, who share the deck hot tub and sauna as well as the most impressive view on the island. Inexpensive to moderate.

Sutil Lodge, Southwind Drive, Galiano, B.C. V0N 1P0, (604) 539-2930. Built in 1928, this guest house with 1930s decor and shared baths is situated at the base of Mount Sutil directly on a sheltered bay and surrounded by twenty private acres of forest. Sumptuous breakfasts are served in the sunny dining area, and lunch and dinner can be arranged. Cozy, tiny cabins along the water's edge are nicely redecorated, and guests have access to canoes and grass tennis courts. Inexpensive to moderate. Owners Ann and Tom

Hennessy are happy to arrange a sailing excursion on their 46-foot catamaran to photograph Seal Rocks, a bird sanctuary, then enjoy a seafood picnic when they drop anchor at a sandy beach.

Woodstone Country Inn, Georgeson Bay Road, R.R. 1, Galiano, B.C. V0N 1P0, (604) 539-2022. Visitors arrive via an English country lane leading to this mansion in the woods. The inn, overlooking a broad meadow where sheep graze near an old barn, offers twelve very comfortable guest rooms, some with fireplaces. Opened in August 1989, the inn takes full advantage of the available light with its high ceilings, large windows, and spacious public rooms. We enjoyed afternoon tea here and moved on reluctantly. Moderate to expensive.

Madrona Lodge, R.R. 2, Galiano, B.C. V0N 1P0, (604) 539-2926. The eleven cedar log housekeeping cottages are located on the northern end of Porlier Pass Drive, where the road meets the sea. This is our favorite part of the island. There's a boat ramp, and rowboats and bicycles are available to rent. Inexpensive to moderate.

The Galiano Tourist Bureau will be happy to send a complete list of cottages and bed and breakfasts. Galiano Island Travel Infocentre, Box 73, Galiano, B.C. V0N 1P0, (604) 639-2233.

WHERE TO EAT

Humming Bird Inn is a friendly pub in Sturdies Bay with inexpensive meals, take-out food, and a picnic area. Located inside the Galiano Market (Sturdies Bay), *Lony's Cozy Café* is a good place to eat in an artistic environment. It offers a menu that changes daily, espressos, a juice bar, and excellent dessert. *Woodstone Country Inn* serves superb four-course dinners with produce from its organically grown garden. Reservations are recommended. Call 539-2022. *Spanish Hills Store*, about 14 miles along Porlier Pass Drive, before the road dead-ends (see map), offers espressos, caffe lattes, and light snacks in an idyllic waterfront setting.

North and South Pender

These are the second largest of the Gulf Islands and the southernmost, lying closest to the U.S. border. Bedwell Harbour, on South Pender, is where foreign vessels clear entry to Canadian waters.

At one time these islands were one, joined by a narrow isthmus between Bedwell and Browning harbours. Indians and early settlers from both islands used to row down to the isthmus, drag their vessels across, and continue to their destination, whether north or south, saving themselves miles of rowing. In 1903, with the arrival of more settlers to the island, the federal government cut a canal through the isthmus wide enough for a small vessel to negotiate; from then on, the two parts were designated "North" and "South." In 1955, the canal bridge linking the two islands was built. It is a one-lane bridge on which cars must give way to each other. No signal has ever been necessary, since there is so little traffic. The road connects the islands, but many of the scenic bays and beaches are accessible only to the sailor or hiker.

Otter Bay Ferry Terminal, entrance to these unique islands, is situated on the north island, which has the larger

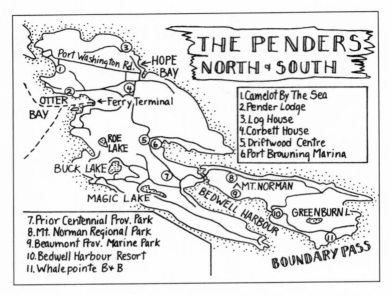

THE PENDERS NORTH & SOUTH

1. Camelot By The Sea
2. Pender Lodge
3. Log House
4. Corbett House
5. Driftwood Centre
6. Port Browning Marina

7. Prior Centennial Prov. Park
8. Mt. Norman Regional Park
9. Beaumont Prov. Marine Park
10. Bedwell Harbour Resort
11. Whalepointe B & B

population. Brett's Bicycle Base is about a thirty-minute walk from the terminal. Beware of the tiring hills! When we bicycled on our first visit, the mid-June heat was so over-whelming (and unusual) that we only made it as far as Pender Lodge, where we sizzled beneath an umbrella on the deck and enjoyed a surprisingly good lunch. Replete and relaxed, all we could do was coast downhill to the ferry. When we returned to the island another day, the weather was perfect.

Turning left at the ferry terminal intersection, we quickly passed Pender Lodge and entered new territory of picturesque farmhouses and abundant orchards and gardens. At Port Washington, we stopped to buy a map at Southridge Feeds, a general store decorated with ancient farm implements and local produce displayed on the front

porch. Inside is a contrast of old-time and modern, with
sacks of horse feed lined up opposite the rows of videos.
Here customers stop to pass the time of day—as they have
for years.

At the end of Port Washington, on the west coast,
Bridge Road runs down to the boat docks. There, by the
water's edge, stands the original general store, built in 1910,
awaiting its next occupants. Neat and tidy old cottages with
ocean views, many with clipped lawns and large orchards,
are nestled near the shore. On the east coast, at Hope Bay,
lies a fishing village, busy with fishermen mending nets and
sprucing up their boats. The majority of the residents on
these islands are retired people who have opted for life
away from the maddening city. Since the Penders are so

BURL WILLES

close to Vancouver Island, more urban services are available than on the rest of the Gulf Islands. A number of residents commute daily to jobs on the mainland.

North Pender has three lakes: Buck, Magic, and Roe. Roe, the smallest, is an hour-long hike; Buck and Magic are accessible by car. Summer brings visitors to these lakes like bees to a honey pot, but the lakes are not polluted.

Greenburn Lake on South Pender is the most remote, accessible by a two-hour hike. It has become somewhat of a wildlife sanctuary, with bald eagles nesting in this area and countless other forest foragers. There are no large animals like bears or cougars.

Driftwood Centre on the main road near Port Browning Marina is where most of the community goes to transact its business. Even the bank, the only bank among all the southern Gulf Islands, has a rustic charm.

Temperatures occasionally soar in the summer, so after a hike or bike ride, a pleasant swim in one of the lakes or coves is a must. Fishing and boating are major recreational activities on the island. You'll see notices about rentals and excursions posted at all the marinas. The best way of discovering North and South Pender's many coves is by canoeing. North Pender has a golf and country club, including a driving range. Scuba services are available at Thieves Bay Marina and tennis at Port Browning Marina.

Prior Centennial Provincial Park on North Pender, around the Magic Lake area, is frequented more by locals than visitors. Beaumont Marine Park is located on the southwest coast of South Pender. It has rugged trails leading from Canal Road to the shores of Bedwell Harbour or over Mount Norman across the east side of Browning Harbour. Camping is permitted in both parks for a nominal fee.

BURL WILLES

Traveling along any of the roads, you will often see small tables with flowers, fruits, and vegetables for sale. Often the owners, working elsewhere, will leave unattended money boxes with change awaiting payment. Such is the easygoing country life on the Penders.

HOW TO GET THERE

Otter Bay, the only ferry terminal for both the Penders, has a ferry run three or four times daily from Swartz Bay and a twice-a-day run from Tsawwassen on Vancouver. For 24-hour recorded schedule information, call B.C. Island Ferries (604) 656-0757 in Victoria and (604) 685-1021 in Vancouver.

WHERE TO STAY

Bedwell Harbour Resort, R.R. 1, South Pender Island, B.C. V0N 2M0, (604) 629-3221. This resort, tucked away on Egeria Bay ten miles from the ferry terminal, offers pickup for ferry passengers. A marina belonging to the resort draws countless foreign yachts. Hotel rooms or housekeeping cottages with fireplaces face the harbor. There is a heated outdoor swimming pool, a restaurant, a pub, a laundry, and a grocery store. Closed November through March. Moderate to expensive.

Pender Lodge, MacKinnon Road, R.R. 1, South Pender Island, B.C. V0N 2M0, (604) 629-3493. Built in the 1920s on five acres of oceanfront property, Pender Lodge offers a choice of rooms in the lodge with shared or private baths or cottages with kitchens. Guests enjoy excellent meals in the dining room or on the deck facing the sea. There is a swimming pool and a tennis court. Moderate to expensive.

Camelot-by-the-Sea, Otter Bay Road, Pender Island, B.C. V0N 2M0, (604) 629-3770. This newly constructed, whimsical, eclectic, Victorian-Gothic mansion has an ideal location steps from a private beach at Grimmer Bay. Moderate to expensive.

Port Browning Marina, Hamilton Road, Pender Island, B.C. V0N 2M0, (604) 629-3493. Facing onto a park-like setting of lawn, trees, and picnic tables plus a long stretch of curving beach, Port Browning Marina's self-contained cabins are ideal for families who enjoy the hum of activity: swimming pool, tennis court, yacht marina, shops, boat and bicycle rentals, and an indoor/outdoor restaurant. Moderate.

BURL WILLES

WHERE TO EAT

Driftwood Café near Port Browning Marina in the Driftwood Shopping Center serves light lunches and dinners
with an espresso bar and soup and sandwich menu. Outdoor seating is available in good weather. *Eagle Nest Restaurant*, located in Pender Lodge and open to the public,
offers a varied menu, with homegrown vegetables and
locally produced meats. Reservations are recommended
for dinner (tel. 629-3221), but lunch on the newly added
deck is more informal. *Port Browning Marina* serves good
pub food. Nonsmokers can escape to the outdoor picnic
tables on the deck with scenic view of forest and ocean. Our
fresh salmon sandwich and Caesar salad were delicious.

Saturna

In 1791, Captain José Maria Narvaez of the Spanish naval schooner *Saturnia* gave the island its name. Saturna is considered by the locals to be the "dark isle" of the Mayne, Pender, Galiano group. The mystery surrounding Saturna can be attributed partly to the limited number of ferry calls to the island and the general isolation that one feels once there. Possibly this is because there are only 350 permanent residents for the 31 square kilometers of land. The few roads on Saturna are narrow and tree lined and in many areas covered by a thick canopy of leaves. These perpetually shaded thoroughfares add to the secretiveness of the island.

A valley runs from Lyall Harbour to Narvaez Bay in an east/west direction. Two mountain ridges run down the northern and southern sides. The southern slopes of these ridges are extremely steep. Notable peaks on the northern ridge are Mount David and Mount Elford. Mount Warburton Pike on the southern ridge, with an elevation of 490 meters, is the highest peak on the island.

Saturna is the largest island in the group and the least populated. Its small population, mostly concentrated on the western side, forms a tight community that manages to produce summer theater, the fall fair, picnics, dances, and what is perhaps the most widely known and special event, the July 1st lamb barbecue, held annually on the beach since 1950, whatever the weather. Visitors are warmly welcome to join in the celebration, which continues until dusk—around 9:00 p.m. at that time of year.

Take a hike on Mount Warburton Pike. The southern slopes of this mountain ridge afford excellent views of

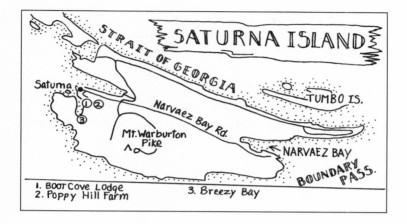

1. Boot Cove Lodge
2. Poppy Hill Farm
3. Breezy Bay

Pender, Mayne, and other Gulf Islands, Vancouver Island, and the San Juans. The slopes of this ridge are steep, and during the summer months the grasses covering the area turn a bright beige, making a sharp contrast to the surrounding greens and blues. On windy days, the sounds of screaming ravens riding the updrafts mingle with the sounds of the forest, creating a supernatural energy. During calmer weather, you may be lucky enough to see feral goats grazing here, descendants of the early settlers' domestic animals gone wild. A wildlife sanctuary near the south side of East Point, a provincial park at Winter Cove, and an ecological reserve near the top of Mount Warburton Pike are recommended by locals.

Most of Saturna's roads are suitable for hiking and cycling as traffic is usually light year-round. One stretch that is particularly scenic is East Point Road leading out to the lighthouse. The road follows the seashore of Tumbo Channel and has a number of beach accesses. The trees lining the sides have sculptural trunk formations. The dense ground foliage consists of salal, blackberry, Oregon grape, and sword ferns. East Point itself is excellent for observing a large variety of seabirds, otters, seals, and sea lions; also, during the summer months whales can be seen from the point. To the left of the lighthouse is a dirt road (foot traffic only) that quickly leads down to a pleasant small beach with crystal clear shallow water. We came prepared with a picnic lunch. (There are *no* Galiano Market cafés on Saturna!)

Narvaez Bay is another good beach to walk along, and this area is a popular place to see deer. Boot Cove Road and Payne Road, both near the ferry pier, are pretty, woods-edged roads well worth a stroll or drive.

The island residents, though friendly, remain somewhat indifferent to the tourist traffic. Tourism does exacerbate the lack of water. In almost every yard you will see giant blue and white plastic containers meant to gather rain water for household use. All nonbiodegradable litter has to be carted away on the ferry. Residents have learned to recycle, and nearly everyone has a compost pile.

Homesteading has been the norm on this island. Log houses are a common sight. Residents raise a large amount of garden produce, using twelve-foot fences to ward off the deer.

Jon and Priscilla run Haggis Farms, a bakery that fronts the road several miles from the ferry dock. Jon is known everywhere since once a week he does a bread run in his little diesel boat, making deliveries to the neighboring islands, including Victoria and Vancouver. When we stopped to say hello, we found only Priscilla, who was working in

BURL WILLES

her abundant vegetable and flower garden. Priscilla's garden never ceases to show off its colors during the changing seasons. Bread-making day, she says, often requires twenty-three or twenty-four hours of nonstop work. Somehow they also manage to tend their many farm animals. An astronomical amount of energy to most people is all in a day's work to them. We left with a gift bag of crisp, juicy Gravenstein apples, the best we've ever tasted. They never made it back to Mayne Island but were consumed between Haggis Farm and the ferry dock.

HOW TO GET THERE

Ferries run to Lyall Harbour from Swartz Bay and Tsawwassen but less frequently than to the other Gulf Islands. Visitors should check schedules carefully for sailing times. For 24-hour recorded schedule information, call B.C. Island Ferries (604) 656-0757 in Victoria and (604) 685-1021 in Vancouver.

WHERE TO STAY

There are very few places available for overnight accommodation on Saturna, so a reservation is a necessity during the summer months, especially on weekends. We calculated that thirty-eight was the largest number that could be accommodated overnight, not including the very few cabins and rental houses available.

Boot Cove Lodge and Restaurant, Payne Road, P.O. Box 54, Saturna Island, B.C. V0N 2Y0, (604) 539-2254. One mile from the ferry terminal and overlooking a pic-

BURL WILLES

turesque cove, the Boot Cove Lodge was being rebuilt when we were there. After a major renovation, the lodge now has more sun exposure and rooms facing the sea. Quiet, with a view of the surrounding bay. Moderate.

Breezy Bay, Payne Road, P.O. Box 40, Saturna Island, B.C. V0N 2Y0, (604) 539-2937. There are four comfortable rooms for rent in this historic farmhouse nestled in twenty-eight acres. There is a library and a private beach. Dinner can be arranged. Inexpensive.

Poppy Hill Farm, 104 Payne Road, P.O. Box 44, Saturna Island, B.C. V0N 2Y0, (604) 539-5002. Friendly Janet Comstock welcomes travelers to her Poppy Hill Farm. The large double room upstairs (360 square feet) with private bath has an ocean view and is a bargain. Downstairs is one double room with shared bath and a tiny single at a very reasonable rate. Inexpensive.

East Point Resort, East Point Road, Saturna Island, B.C. V0N 2Y0, (604) 539-2975. Situated above a small sandy beach near the East Point Lighthouse, these are spacious housekeeping units with full kitchens, one or two bedrooms, and deck. One week minimum stay in July and August. Moderate.

WHERE TO EAT

One of the two eating establishments on the island is *Boot Cove Restaurant*. Reservations are recommended as the menu changes daily and meals are cooked to order. Telephone (604) 539-2254. Inexpensive *Lyall Harbour Pub* has a deck over the water for hot summer days. This is an ideal spot to watch the ferry arrive or the school water taxi bring the local children home from a neighboring island. Crews from foreign vessels that anchor off Plumper Sound waiting for entry into Vancouver often spend their shore time here.

WASHINGTON

San Juan Islands

We approached the San Juan Islands from Canada, taking the daily ferry from the attractive harbor town of Sidney, on Vancouver Island north of Victoria. As the ferry swung majestically south, we were impressed once again with the vast expanses of this watery world, in which the islands seem almost incidental little parcels of land subdued and clung to in the face of the ongoing, indifferent beauty and majesty of the surrounding mountains and waterways. In the warmer months, the boats are impressive, too, in their number and variety; we thought about the Indian canoes and Spanish galleons that plied these waters a very short time ago and wondered what the next few hundred years might bring.

The big stately ferry sliding through the water is such a grand, slow ride that it is almost as if the ship were standing still and a film of the beautiful scenery were being reeled past the lounge windows. We're spectators, we're sleepy, we're leaving the city behind to go where light rises from the water, where whales frolic and bald eagles fly overhead like crows.

There are 172 islands in this archipelago lying between Washington State and Vancouver Island. Only four are

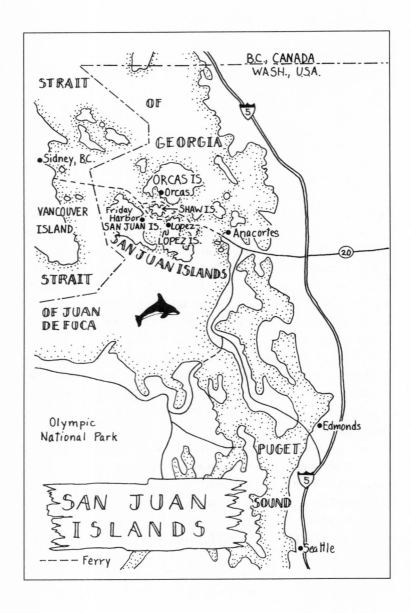

served by the ferries, a few more are inhabited by those who can travel by private plane or boat, several are protected wildlife reserves. They enjoy a gentler climate than the mainland—about half the annual rainfall—due to the "rain shadow" of the Olympic mountains.

The islands were originally occupied by Indians. Early settlers farmed: fruit was a major crop until the shipping costs made it noncompetitive (one of the delectable sights in springtime is old fruit trees flowering everywhere you turn). There are still farms on the islands, along with an increasing number of vacation and weekend retreats. These do not dominate the landscape but are tucked in among the trees and coves. You can see those along the shoreline best from the water; some of them are little Valhallas. People also retire here. The islands are home to artists and craftspeople, and some of the residents work off-island part of the time. Not far from the growing city of Seattle, the San Juans serve as a weekend escape hatch for urbanites.

This makes for a lot of coming and going. When you travel from one island to the next, it's best to arrive at the ferry landing fifteen to twenty minutes before departure time, earlier during the busier times of year. Park your car in the lane clearly marked for your island destination and purchase a ticket from the ticket agent. There's a big ferry that makes the Anacortes, Washington/Sidney, B.C. run once daily, more often in summer, as well as smaller boats that run interisland from Anacortes.

If you start from Sidney, B.C., you are requested to arrive at the ferry 1½ hours before boarding because you must clear customs and immigration, but we've never experienced a briefer or more painless border crossing. You can leave your car in line and take a brief stroll around the spanking new Sidney Harbour pleasure boat marina, just a few blocks away. On your left as you walk out on the marina, note the oak frames, red cedar planking, and complex rigging of the old sailboat *Dorothy,* built in 1897. Nearby, Pelicano's Coffee Shop and Bakery looks like a good bet for quick refreshments. Next door to it, overlooking the harbor, is the Rumrunner, a fully licensed restaurant whose name gives you an idea of what used to go on in this harbor. And don't miss the brand-new Sidney Museum, which has attractive displays featuring clear, detailed information about whales, as well as a room full of old farm implements and photographs from the region. Open daily May to Labor Day, 10:00 a.m. to 4:00 p.m. For other times, call 656-1322. Admission is by donation.

Only four of the islands are accessible by ferry: San Juan, Orcas, Lopez, and Shaw, but many more are accessible by private boat and some by plane as well. For a thorough discussion of the boating possibilities in the San Juans, we highly recommend *The San Juan Islands Afoot and Afloat*, by Marge and Ted Mueller (Seattle: The Mountaineers, 1988).

San Juan

Friday Harbor, on San Juan Island, is the county seat and commercial hub of the San Juan Islands. Before we arrived, we heard a little grumbling about how touristy it has become. True, it's full of restaurants and has a tiny parking problem, an art gallery with paintings by the resident novelist Ernest K. Gann, and a couple of fancy jewelry stores

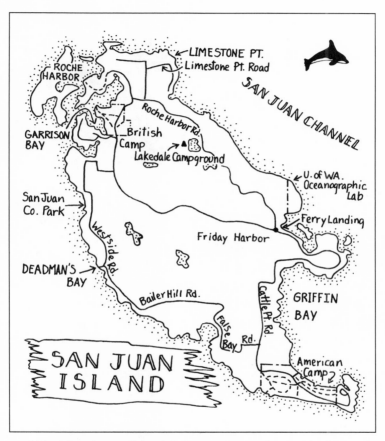

and T-shirt shops, but this is not Carmel or Sausalito; it's still basically a small island town serving a rural population.

We like three spots in Friday Harbor that haven't succumbed to the wave of self-consciousness that sometimes washes over towns like this. They are all on Spring Street, the main drag. The Friday Harbor Drug Store is like a vast, old-fashioned five-and-dime with anything you could

LINDA LANCIONE MOYER

wish for in stock, including postcards, stamps, and island cookbooks. Herb's Tavern on the corner exudes a beery smell and looks like it's been there forever, as does the Donut Shop, where you will find fluorescent lights, formica tables, a bottomless cup of coffee, and old-timers in cowboy hats giving the waitresses a hard time.

In contrast, if progress is measured by the number of espresso machines, Friday Harbor is way ahead of its time, with eight in a five-block radius, according to Glenn Stewart, owner of one of them. Stewart is the proprietor of Stewart's, an old house on Spring Street that he has converted into a charming refuge for coffee and book lovers. There's a fireplace and small tables in both the upstairs and downstairs rooms, where you can pull one of the used books for sale off the shelf and read while you drink your coffee or tea. The collection includes everything from antique print media such as newspapers dating from the Civil and Revolutionary wars to romance novels. He also offers for sale handmade braided rugs from Canada, the official poster of the Washington State Ferry system, and tapes from Nature Recordings, a company based on the island for which his wife is the sound engineer. A room upstairs is available for local businesses and churches to hold meetings (or astrological readings, as the case may be). We can think of no place we'd rather spend a rainy afternoon in the Northwest than sitting in an upstairs front room in a velvet wing chair sipping a cappuccino and reading an old novel.

Despite being the commercial hub of San Juan County, the word that most frequently comes to mind on San Juan outside of Friday Harbor is *pastoral*. Driving past pretty farmhouses in spring, sunlight breaking through the lowering clouds and the trees just coming into leaf, we felt like we were in an English landscape painting.

LINDA LANCIONE MOYER

Indeed, but for the twists and turns of history, we might well have been in a British outpost, for in the nineteenth century, ownership of the midchannel territory between Vancouver Island and the mainland was disputed by Britain and the United States. The Hudson Bay Company laid claim to the island, as did the Oregon Territorial Legislature, which governed what is now the state of Washington. A confrontation occurred in 1859, when an American settler shot and killed a pig belonging to the Hudson Bay Company. When the British threatened to arrest the man, the Americans demanded military protection. Military forces were mounted on both sides; although no shots were fired, the situation remained a stalemate for twelve years, until the dispute was finally settled through the arbitration of Kaiser Wilhelm I.

This episode, known as the Pig War, is commemorated on San Juan by a National Historic Park, which consists of British Camp, at the north end of the island, and American Camp, near Friday Harbor. Both have self-guided trails describing the event that took place there. In American Camp, you can hike to the top of Mount Finlayson, where on a clear day you can see Mount Baker, Mount Rainier, the Olympic Mountains, and British Columbia. You can also walk along South Beach, the longest public beach on the island. In British Camp, your hiking options are the fairly level trail to Bull Point or the steep trail to the British cemetery and the top of Young Hill. Both parks are for day use only; no camping.

Circling the island by car is a trip of an hour or two or a day, depending on how long you linger. Going south of Friday Harbor, stop at American Camp, then drive through

LINDA LANCIONE MOYER

pretty, flat farm country where there are many photogenic houses until you reach the sunnier side of the island, which is also more barren and windswept than the east side. San Juan County Park is an excellent place for whale watching. The next point of interest is British Camp, described above.

Be sure to drive out to Roche Harbor for a look at Roche Harbor Resort, a handsome old white hotel with verandas which faces the harbor. It is notable for its colorful formal garden and for the fact that on two occasions, Teddy Roosevelt, a friend of the owner, stayed here. His faintly penciled signature can be observed on the guest register, and the room he stayed in is now called the Presidential Suite.

On the Fourth of July, boats from all over gather in the harbor for the grand fireworks display, the biggest event of the season.

Continuing east from Rochedale you will see a discreet sign pointing toward Giannangelo Farms, an herb farm whose lovely gardens are open to the public from 11:00 a.m. to 5:00 p.m. They sell potpourris, herbal teas, special vinegars, and dried herbs to the public or by mail order.

San Juan is a prosperous island with a growing population. Someone told us there is full employment on the island because of all the construction going on for the newcomers. But the old islanders don't go away. A man who graduated from high school with the class of 1974 told us that 90 percent of the graduates of his class are still on the island. We also met several people who had lived in San Diego or Seattle for many years and returned in middle age to the island where they were born. We can see why.

HOW TO GET THERE

Take Interstate 5 from Seattle or Vancouver, B.C., to Anacortes, approximately a ninety-minute drive. Follow the signs to the Anacortes ferry. The ferry takes about two hours. For schedules, call Washington State Ferry (800) 542-7052 or (800) 542-0810 within Washington State. Outside Washington State: (206) 464-6400. This ferry also calls at least once a day at Sidney, B.C., from where it takes approximately two hours to reach Friday Harbor.

WHERE TO STAY

Roche Harbor Resort, P.O. Box 4001, Roche Harbor, WA 98250, (206) 378-2155. This complex of accommodations includes the Hotel de Haro, some modern condominiums, and the "Company Town cottages." Well-maintained older buildings in a very pleasant setting. Moderate.

Moon and Sixpence, Beaverton Valley Road, Friday Harbor, WA 98250, (206) 378-4138. This turn-of-the-

LINDA LANCIONE MOYER

century dairy farm has five varied guest accommodations with shared and private baths and a family-style Dutch breakfast. Moderate.

Olympic Lights, 4531-A Cattle Point Road, Friday Harbor, WA 98250, (206) 378-3186. This is a splendid old two-story farmhouse with wide verandas situated in an open meadow looking out over sea and mountains. Moderate.

Trumpeter Inn, 420 Trumpeter Way, Friday Harbor, WA 98250, (206) 378-3884. Named after the trumpeter swans that grace the nearby ponds, this inn is an ideal place to enjoy the tranquillity of the island and observe its wildlife. Each of the six rooms has a private bath. Moderate.

States Inn, 2039 West Valley Road, Friday Harbor, WA 98250, (206) 378-6240. This relatively new inn features eight rooms named after states and decorated in the mood of the state. The original building was a schoolhouse, then a ranch house, but it has been completely remodeled. It is located in a valley just south of British Camp. Expensive.

Hillside House, 365 Carter Avenue, Friday Harbor, WA 98250, (206) 378-4730. Each of the six guest rooms at Hillside House has a view of either the harbor or the woods and garden and a cozy window seat to enjoy it from. The proprietors, Dick and Cathy Robinson, suggest leaving your car behind as their place is very close to Friday Harbor and there is taxi service available on the island. Moderate.

A complete listing of bed and breakfasts can be obtained from the Bed and Breakfast Association of San Juan Island, Friday Harbor, WA 98250.

For those who prefer to camp, *Lakedale Campground*, 2627 Roche Harbor Road, Friday Harbor, WA 98250, (206) 378-2350, is our campground of choice on San Juan. It is scrupulously tidy and well run, with over two hundred spacious, tree-filled campsites on an island between two lakes. Fishing and boat rentals are available. Camping at *San Juan State Park* is also good, but campsites are at a premium during whale-watching season. Someone told us after we left the island that the Bistro restaurant on Spring and First has a *hostel* upstairs.

Dockside Property Company, Box 1459, Friday Harbor, WA 98250, (800) 992-1904, handles vacation rentals.

WHERE TO EAT

Springtree Restaurant, located in a pretty setting on Spring Street in downtown Friday Harbor, has a reputation for serving the best food on the island. Reservations are recommended: call 378-4848. Also highly praised by the locals is *Café Bissett* in Friday Harbor, at the corner of First and West. Call 378-3109 for reservations. While some consider the *Duck Soup Inn*, out in the country, to be overpriced, others praise it highly. *Downrigger*, at the harbor, has a broad menu at dinner, and the food is consistent, if a little packaged. At lunch they serve a fine hamburger.

There's a new Chinese place on Spring Street where the food is good, but one local resident complained of long waits and small portions. Check out the Mexican spot on Spring Street, at the back of a little arcade. *Stewart's* offers, in addition to coffees and desserts, an inexpensive lunch that sometimes includes a gumbo prepared by the native Texan owner. He plans to begin serving wine and light meals in the evening soon. An ideal place for an inexpensive family lunch or even a very early supper for campers (they close at 5:00 p.m.) is the *Donut Shop* on Spring Street, where a half portion of taco salad is enough food for anyone. It's also great for high-cholesterol-and-cigarette-smoke breakfasts. Still another spot to eat well and inexpensively is the *Bistro* on Spring and First, which serves sandwiches and deep dish pizza. And finally, we highly recommend the *Front Street Café*, right across from the ferry landing, for its tasty, inexpensive, cafeteria-style breakfasts and delicious baked goods.

Orcas

Orcas Island is shaped rather like a limp butterfly, the two floppy wings divided by a long channel of water known as East Sound. The ferry landing is at Orcas, on the west wing of the island. The tiny town of Orcas consists of a clutch of souvenir shops and a café or two and is the location of the Orcas Hotel, a beautifully restored Victorian Inn.

Drive from Orcas to the village of Eastsound, located at the thinnest part of the island, the base of East Sound. This is the island's main town and includes a supermarket, a good little bookstore, and several restaurants as well as the usual browsers boutiques that spring up in such places. The tiny museum is open only in summer. There's enough to keep you busy in the village for an hour or two, but the real charms of Orcas lie in its varied terrain and its spectacular coastline.

For some of the best of the natural world on Orcas, visit Moran State Park, which encompasses nearly 4,700 acres, including two mountains and five lakes. The original park was once owned by Robert Moran, shipbuilder and mayor of Seattle in the 1920s. We walked around Mountain Lake on a beautiful, tree-lined trail about six miles long, witnessing the result of the two severe winter windstorms of 1991, which according to a ranger, felled an estimated 30,000 trees. Logs were strewn everywhere like toothpicks. Light glistened on the beads of sap on the newly fallen trees, and we drowned in the scent of cut cedar. Someone pointed out to us that although devastating, the destruction that accompanies such a violent storm brings with it a natural renewal as more light floods into the forest and fosters new growth.

From the WPA-built stone observation tower atop Mount Constitution, the highest point in the San Juans, there are excellent views of the surroundings islands, as well as Anacortes, Billingham, Mount Baker, and Vancouver. You can drive up to the top or brave the steep hiking trail.

Don't miss the famous Rosario Resort. The main building is the former mansion of Robert Moran, donor of the

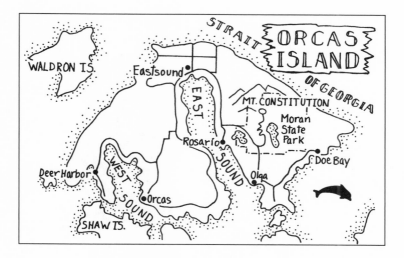

original Moran park, who, the story has it, came to Orcas thinking he had only two years to live and survived another forty. Moran envisioned his family home as an opulent oceanliner, sleek and white, with brass railings and handsome woodwork in mahogany and teak. Visitors are free to wander around among the family portraits hung downstairs or go upstairs to the music room, complete with pipe organ and stained glass windows, where evening performances are often open to the public. Downstairs is a spa with a workout room, sauna, boutique, and pool, which is notable for the original floors set with tiny colored tiles in pretty patterns.

We love the contrast between this resort and another one farther down the road at Doe Bay. If Rosario is a little too stuffy and opulent for your taste, you'll get a kick out of the tie-dyed flag hoisted over the water at Doe Bay. Cowabunga, we're back in the sixties, with a natural foods res-

LINDA LANCIONE MOYER

taurant, a motley assortment of accommodations, and the best part—a mineral bath hot tub, swimsuit optional, that overlooks the sound and has a pretty little waterfall tumbling by it. Sea kayaking excursions in two-person kayaks with experienced guides depart from here and are highly recommended. When there's a full moon, they sometimes even go out at midnight.

Before coming to Doe Bay, you'll breeze past the little town of Olga. Be sure to stop at the Orcas Island Artworks and Café Olga, a cooperative gallery of local arts and crafts representing over seventy Orcas Island artists. Here you'll find high-quality weaving, ceramics, jewelry, and beeswax candles beautifully displayed in a light airy space that in its former life was used for strawberry barreling. At the Café Olga, in one corner of the building, you can hang out with a book all afternoon debating which of the fabulous des-

LINDA LANCIONE MOYER

serts to try next. Upstairs is Nebula, a small New Age book-store that has some intriguing large quartz crystal bowls. When the rim is circled with a rubber mallet, they send off wave after wave of an astonishing reverberating sound.

On the less-visited part of the island, the drive from Westsound to Deer Harbor along the shoreline is one of the most scenic.

HOW TO GET THERE

Take the ferry from Anacortes, Washington, or Sidney, B.C. Or fly from Seattle Sea-Tac Airport on Chart Air or from downtown Seattle via seaplane on Lake Union Air, which offers free transportation from their downtown Seattle ter-minals to the airport.

WHERE TO STAY

Turtleback Farm Inn, Route 1, Box 650, Eastsound, WA 98245, (206) 376-4914. This elegant inn, a refurbished and expanded farmhouse with seven beautifully appointed rooms, overlooks forest and farmland. It is located in Crow Valley six miles from the ferry landing. In addition to a full breakfast, coffee and tea are available for guests throughout the day, and sherry is offered in the evening. Expensive.

Sand Dollar Inn, P.O. Box 152, Olga, WA 98279, (206) 376-5696. Overlooking Buck Bay in the tiny town of Olga, this inn offers four pleasant rooms (three with views) and a full breakfast at moderate prices.

Outlook Inn, P.O. Box 210, Eastsound, WA 98245, (206) 376-2200. Located in a grand old white building in East-sound overlooking the water, the inn dates from 1888, when it served the tradesmen who arrived by boat to buy island fruit. There are nineteen rooms furnished in turn-of-the-century style in the main building, all but one with shared bath, and ten additional rooms in a newer structure which have private baths, phones, and television. Inexpensive/moderate.

Orcas Hotel, P.O. Box 155, Orcas, WA 98280, (206) 376-4300. Convenient to the ferry landing, this beautifully restored 91-year-old hotel is impeccably clean and quiet and offers such special touches as beautifully ironed linens and a choice of breakfast buffet-style or served in your room. Some rooms have shared baths, some have jacuzzis.

Rosario, One Rosario Way, Eastsound, WA 98245-2222, (206) 376-2222. A nationally known resort, Rosario is listed on the National Register of Historic Places. Tasteful modern units near the mansion overlook the bay. Expensive.

LINDA LANCIONE MOYER

Doe Bay Village Resort and Retreat, 86 Star Route, Olga, WA 98279, (206) 376-4755. Very rustic waterfront cabins (shared shower and kitchen), camping at spectacular campsites with some water views, and a large hostel at the water's edge (a converted boat house) offer a variety of choices. Inexpensive.

Moran State Park, Star Route 22, Eastsound, WA 98245, (206) 376-2326. This park has 151 campsites. The ones we saw were spacious and wooded. Three of the park's eight comfort stations have hot showers.

This is only a partial listing of accommodations on Orcas. A-1 Room Service, P.O. Box 697, Eastsound, WA 98245, (206) 376-5889, can refer you to accommodations in private homes.

LINDA LANCIONE MOYER

WHERE TO EAT

In Eastsound, *Christina's*, on the waterfront, has an excellent reputation. *Bilbo's* serves great Mexican food and *La Famiglia* serves hearty Italian food, including pizza. In addition, there are several other restaurants to choose from. Outside of town, *Rosario* is known for its Sunday brunch and Friday evening seafood buffet. We love the food at *Café Olga*, where the menu changes daily and there are almost always three wonderful homemade soups. Try their Sicilian artichoke pie and their desserts. Unfortunately, Café Olga closes at 6:00 p.m. In season, *Doe Bay Resort* runs its own natural foods restaurant; if the fresh-baked scones and strong coffee we had the first morning they opened for the season are any indication, it should be fine. The restaurant at *Deer Harbor Resort* is reputedly good.

Lopez

On Lopez we wondered if we should put the house on the market and kiss the city good-bye. Could we find happiness growing old roses around a farmhouse fence and looking out over a meadow at the sunset? And were there still farmhouses left to buy? Lopez has more of a rural farm, less of a country-life-and-leisure feeling than the other San Juans we visited. There are still many working farms here, and cows graze freely along the roadside. If you're driving, likely as not you'll find yourself following a pickup truck carrying a bale of hay. And local residents still lift the hand off the steering wheel in a laconic wave as you drive past.

Lopez is an island perfectly geared, excuse us, for cyclists. It's flatter than either San Juan or Orcas, and some cyclists we met told us that there are twelve cycling rest stops located at strategic scenic places around the island.

To reach Lopez Village, proceed from the ferry landing along Fisherman Bay Road. The main part of the village is off to your right opposite the old red schoolhouse that serves as a library building; we drove right past it the first time around. On your right as you drive into town is the Lopez Village Market. The day we were there, fresh cooked shrimp was being sold by the pound off a truck in the parking lot. Next to the market is Gail's Restaurant, where you can linger over a bowl of shellfish chowder or a Reuben sandwich and watch the town go by. Near Gail's is Panda Books, a small bookstore with a good selection of children's books and an excellent selection of books about the Pacific Northwest. Across the street is an island-sized mall of shops with a café, art gallery, natural food store, and barber shop. The

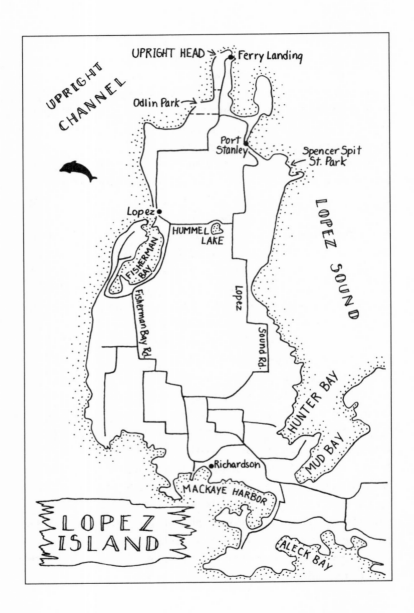

UPRIGHT HEAD
Ferry Landing

UPRIGHT CHANNEL

Odlin Park

Port Stanley

Spencer Spit St. Park

Lopez

HUMMEL LAKE

LOPEZ SOUND

FISHERMAN BAY

Fisherman Bay Rd.

Lopez

Sound Rd.

HUNTER BAY

MUD BAY

Richardson

MACKAYE HARBOR

ALECK BAY

LOPEZ ISLAND

art gallery, Chimera, is a co-op of fifteen artists showing blown glass, beadwork, pottery, and handspun yarns. Farther down on your left is an intriguing-looking restaurant called the Bay Café. As you drive back out of town, note the handsome white church on the right and the substantial red and white library building, with its pretty garden, on Fisherman's Bay Road. The nineteenth-century library building was originally the first school on Lopez.

HOW TO GET THERE

Take the ferry that runs through the San Juans from either Anacortes, Washington, or Sidney, B.C. Two floatplane companies, Kenmore/Air Harbor and Lake Union Air, have scheduled daily service to and from Seattle. Air San Juan/Chart Air, based in Friday Harbor, flies from Lopez airport to Seattle, Bellingham, and Anacortes, as well as between islands. West Isle Air, based in Anacortes, also has daily scheduled service interisland.

WHERE TO STAY

Inn at Swift's Bay, Port Stanley Road, Lopez Island, WA 98261, (206) 468-3636. This place has elegant rooms, elegant breakfasts, and charming hosts. Moderate.

Edenwild Inn, P.O. Box 271, Lopez Island, WA 98261 (206) 468-3238. This newly built, Victorian farmhouse-style inn right in Lopez Village still needs a little landscaping to make it look inviting, but it certainly has some elegant touches, including the many beveled glass windows made by a local glass cutter and beautiful pale gray hardwood floors. The rooms, some with fireplaces, are spacious and airy. Moderate/expensive.

Blue Fjord Cabins, Rt. 1, Box 1450, Lopez Island, WA 98261, (206) 468-2749. Located at the end of an unmarked dirt road, these especially secluded cabins near the water are ideal for those who really want to get far away. Inexpensive/moderate.

There is good camping both at *Spenser Spit State Park*, where the campsites are right on the beach, and *Odlin Park*, near the ferry terminal.

WHERE TO EAT

Gail's Restaurant, in Lopez Village, has a choice of soups, salads, sandwiches, and fresh shellfish dishes served in a pleasant many-windowed room. We had a terrific shellfish chowder and a not-so-hot "Greek pizza" made with phyllo dough (a dish that can be dismissed along with Mexican

LINDA LANCIONE MOYER

LINDA LANCIONE MOYER

quiche). There are local watercolors on display and classi-
cal music on the radio. Why did this place remind us of a
suburban lunchroom? Washington wines, local island mus-
tards, jams, and the like, are for sale.

Because of its name, we expected the *Wildflower
Café*, open from 8:00 a.m. to 8:00 p.m., to offer up lots of
tofu and sprouts and were surprised to find instead pizza,
fish and chips, and burgers, along with such entrées as
salmon steak and teriyaki chicken. Inexpensive.

Shaw

Shaw is the smallest of the four San Juan Islands served by
the ferries. First we heard that an order of Franciscan nuns
operates the ferry landing, then that there are two other

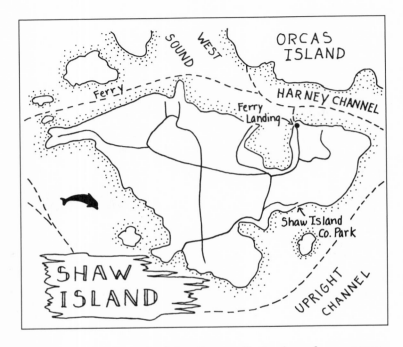

orders of nuns on the island as well. A place for contemplation rather than tourism, we surmised, and decided that a glimpse of a nun operating the bridge at the ferry landing would suffice for our purposes. We were disappointed to see a young man in charge on the day we docked there but noted that the nearby store is charmingly named Little Portion. There are twelve campsites in the county park and no restaurants on the island. If you really want a retreat, go to Shaw.

OREGON

Islands, in Oregon? We sailed along the entire Oregon coast and saw only rocks, but our Portland friend, Barbara Stross, told us not to overlook two island gems, Sauvie and Ross in the Willamette River.

Historic Sauvie Island is an enchanting rural retreat of farms, wildlife, prairies, and quiet country roads overlooked by motorists rushing along Route 30 just north of Portland. We were glad that Barbara encouraged us to linger on this "island in time" and savor its special charm.

Ross Island is actually within the city limits of Portland, very close to the western shore of the Willamette, yet it remains as undiscovered as any more remote island we visited. The entire island is a wildlife preserve, a nature lover's dream, completely devoid of any commercial development or building. It is a flat, quiet haven for those lucky enough to live in Portland and for those seeking a day's outing while visiting there.

It is easy to fall under the spell of Oregon, a unique state of hospitable, friendly people who preserve and respect their magnificent natural heritage of beaches, mountains, lakes, *and* islands for all to enjoy.

Sauvie

Our Dutch friend goes to Sauvie Island when he gets home-sick. It's close to Portland, about ten miles from down-town, and borders the Multnomah Channel on one side and the Columbia River on the other, with its east end at the intersection of the Willamette and the Columbia. Sauvie Island is named for an early French Canadian, Laurent Sauvé, who managed the Hudson Bay Company's dairy operations there. Before the arrival of the white settlers, several tribes of Multnomah Indians lived peacefully on the island for centuries, fishing for salmon and sturgeon, hunt-ing, and gathering edible plants. Lewis and Clark called it Wappato Island, using the Indian word for the wild, potato-like tuber that grew abundantly in ponds and marshes. Har-vested by the women from specially made canoes and usu-ally dried, the wappato root was a staple food and a valuable item of trade.

To reach the island, take Highway 30 toward Astoria, and turn off and cross a short bridge over the channel. The island is lush and calm, a low flat expanse of fields in bloom and a sky that is very clear and very close. Traveling by boat, you can anchor offshore or beach it on the Columbia side. There are no public gas docks, moorages, or boat ramps. The houseboats lining the channel are not for rent. There is nothing to cater to the usual tourist market—not a sin-gle hotel, motel, or restaurant. Multistory buildings, neon signs, and automatic traffic signals are nonexistent. Paved streets are limited, and major roads dead-end in a protected wildlife area of over 12,000 acres. Sauvie Island Road par-allels Multnomah Channel, leading to the west side. Reeder

Road goes east, and Oak Island Road enters the central wildlife lands.

Turn left off the bridge and follow Sauvie Island Road about half a mile for a visit to the old Bybee-Howell House, centerpiece of the Howell Territorial Park. Built around 1855 on 640 acres of an original land claim, the house has been beautifully restored. It's open to the public between June and September, from 10:00 a.m. to 5:00 p.m. It was the first home in Oregon made of plaster, with materials

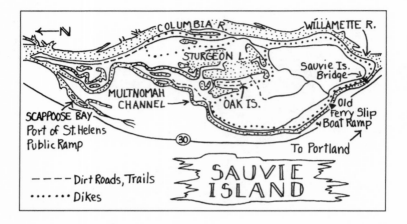

shipped by sail around the Cape of Good Hope from New York. Behind it, in a more recent barn, the Children's Agricultural Museum has a display of farm tools and techniques used during the last 150 years by local settlers.

There are more than one hundred acres of park property now. With careful pruning, replanting, and transplanting of native flora, volunteers from local plant societies have cultivated a wonderful garden and orchard filled with an enormous variety of flowers, shrubs, and trees. Almost 160 different varieties of fruit trees found in early Oregon orchards have been grafted onto dwarfing rootstocks and bear plentifully. The apples are sun warmed and sweet in late summer, and if you want to sample a couple of the delicious windfalls, no one objects. A bog area not far away is deep with camas lily, skunk cabbage, wappato, red osier dogwood, and pussy willow. The frogs and birds love it here. Several picnic tables behind the house allow you to enjoy a leisurely lunch in the century-old setting.

Bicyclists and pedestrians have an easy, level trip across the island on Reeder Road. There aren't many cars except on hot summer weekends. It's all open fields, healthy crops, and grazing cattle. It's peaceful—and quiet enough to notice how noisy and numerous the birds are.

The most dedicated visitors are probably the bird-watchers, who come frequently because the island is a main stopover for migrating flocks and a permanent residence for many birds rarely seen elsewhere locally. Over 250 species of birds, including sandhill cranes, great blue herons, and ring-necked pheasants, live or visit here every year. Sturgeon Lake, at the end of Oak Island Road, is bordered by a mile-long hiking trail from which to watch the waterfowl unobtrusively.

BARBARA STROSS

Lots of mammals, about thirty-seven species, share the territory. Raccoon, red fox, and black-tailed deer are among the most common. All twelve species of amphibians and reptiles are harmless except to the insects and small rodents they eat. Warm-water game fish are easy to spot in the creeks, sloughs, and lakes.

There are enough small waterways for every fisherman to have a private hole. Hunters have access as well. Two sections of marshland (closed during waterfowl season) provide a perfect terrain for training dogs to hunt and retrieve game. The Oregon Department of Fish and Wildlife plants about 1,000 acres of grain crops every year to provide foliage and food for wildlife.

Formed on the floodplain of two major rivers, Sauvie Island began as an accumulation of gravel, sand, and silt. Over the years, floodwaters created many midisland shallow lakes and marshes with interconnecting sloughs, streams, and channels. Seen from the air, it resembles some gigantic unfinished mudpie. Sturgeon Lake is clearly the largest lake, although its contours shift with the seasons. Oak Island, at one end, becomes a boot-shaped peninsula during the summer and is a popular spot for swimming and waterskiing. The land is more stable now than it used to be because, as in Holland, diking has limited many of the natural seasonal overflows, although water levels in several of the wetland areas fluctuate daily with the Columbia River tides. The first dikes, built in the 1920s and 1930s, were washed away in floods that ruined crops and stranded livestock upstairs in their owners' homes. In 1948, the new "Big Dike" barely withstood another annual freshet that peaked at fifteen feet above flood stage.

BARBARA STROSS

The beaches are sandy, shallow, sloping, and safe for swimming. Summer brings crowds, but they're not overwhelming and everyone's relaxed. Fishermen, like birdwatchers, are regulars in every season. The best spots for sand and swimming are on the Columbia side, where there are several privately owned beaches with a small charge for entry per vehicle. Public beaches, on the same side going as far north as Reeder Road goes, are just as pleasant and include an area for nude bathing. Picnicking, walking, swimming, and sunning (on the right day) are all easy to enjoy. But don't count on finding a convenience store for your lunch. There aren't any. Bring it with you, or, better yet, buy just-picked seasonal fruits and vegetables at any of several local farm produce stands. When you sit down to eat, if you haven't already noticed, you'll probably be impressed with the busy marine traffic. Boat watchers see everything from kayaks to containerships, with about as many types of sailing rigs as there are different ducks.

Getting to the northernmost end is an enjoyable three-mile beach hike. There, just beyond a deserted and neglected lighthouse, is a beach loaded with bricks. A collector can find samples stamped with the maker's name, many from Britain. Formerly used in foundries, then as ballast for ships during the Second World War, the bricks were finally dumped in the then-busy shipyard. Now the only evidence of all that industry are several rusting girders, a few well-barnacled and fast-eroding pilings, and, everywhere, the bricks.

Heading back, there's a wooded trail wide enough to have been used as a road at one time but now overgrown and apparently deserted except for the birds on every tree. It's a pleasant walk, easy on the feet and good for the spirit.

Ross

A public boat launch in Willamette Park on the west bank of the river is across from the upper end of Ross Island, so it is easy to reach by water. A good swimmer could make the same crossing, but the current changes that accompany the ocean's tides even this far upstream are surprisingly strong and could cause problems. Even though it is close, few boaters stop off on Ross Island. They waterski, jet boat, sail, canoe, row, paddle, and slowly cruise this stretch of the Willamette most of the summer, noticing the islands mainly to avoid them.

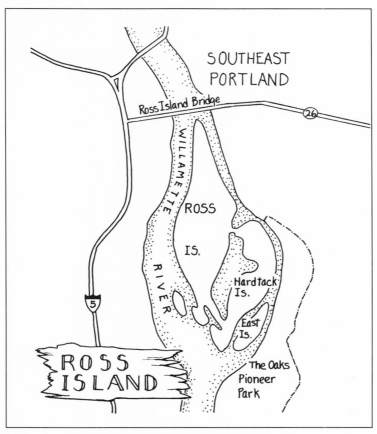

Ross Island is quite a bit closer to the east bank than to the west, an easier approach for the swimmer across a quiet and narrow channel. Along the east side of the Willamette from the Ross Island Bridge almost to the Sellwood Bridge, beyond the island, is Oaks Bottom Wildlife Refuge. It's a good three-quarters of a mile from the nearest street to the river. People come here to fish, walk, bird-watch, plant trees, and put up bat boxes (a project intended to encourage bats to settle in the area) but rarely to swim across the channel.

So Ross Island remains rather quiet and isolated on its west side, mostly thick trees and tangled shrubbery except at the south end, where a wide strip of sandy beach and a small sandy cove around the corner provide a perfect spot for games, naps, picnics, or a small camp fire. The slope from the beach into the water is gradual in most places, and the chilly water feels good on a hot day. Small translucent agates are scattered around. Routine dredging performed for commercial river traffic upstream to Oregon City ensures a frequent turnover of interesting minerals and pebbles on the beach.

The entire island is a wildlife preserve. Great blue heron nest here and feed in Oaks Bottom. They are beautiful birds and easy to identify with their curved necks and impressive wingspan. Owls live here, too. Beaver, deer, and muskrat are more reclusive, living in the vicinity but out of sight. At one time, when growing numbers of rabbits threatened to strip protective ground cover, two foxes, Frieda and Fred, were transplanted to the island. Their presence maintains a stable mammal population. Numerous waterfowl, including various ducks and Canada geese, frequent the extended marshes in Oaks Bottom and make side trips to Ross Island.

Western Oregon has attracted a number of talented ceramic artists who dig their own clay and glaze materials from several good sites. Ross Island is a fine source of clay as well as sand and gravel. Relatively few potters have used this clay, which is light red and so fine grained that it should be mixed with a coarser grit for sculpture work. But sand and gravel have been mined and sold for years by Ross

BARBARA STROSS

Island Sand and Gravel Company, corporate owner of the island. What appears to be an enormous bay is the site of dredging operations. It looks as if a stretch of land on the east side has been excavated almost completely through to the other side. And certainly the bay all but splits the north and south ends completely apart. But what actually happened is quite different. What seems to be one island, what people call Ross Island, used to be two distinct bodies of land separated by a channel whose southwest end was quite narrow. Not all summer sailors are careful navigators, and several accidents raised concern for boating safety, especially with dredging equipment sharing the passage. So Ross Island Sand and Gravel built a land bridge between Ross

Island, the northwesterly island, and Hardhack, its south-easterly companion. It was planted with trees and shrubs to hold the soil and now links the two islands seamlessly.

Hardhack, named for its flourishing *Spiraea douglasii* but commonly misnamed Hardtack Island on maps, has all but lost its identity these days. Hardhack gives Ross Island its most accessible and attractive shore, with a sandy beach, a pleasant cove, and flowering shrubbery on its south end.

Without dikes or other breakwaters, islands in the Willamette seem to shrink in winter when rain swells the river. The effect is more noticeable where seawalls channel its width so that a change in volume acts directly on its depth. In summer, some islands are merely a wade away from shore or actually connected by a spit of land. Ross keeps its distance from riverbanks, but during low-water seasons, the passage on the south across to its tiny neighbor, East Island, is an easy fording. Then, at low tide the waterway may be only a collection of puddles where boats occasionally run aground. Some may be pushed and floated free with the next tide; others must be towed loose.

The southwestern tip of the island pair was our base camp for a week's sailing several summers ago. After sundown it was dark enough to see a sky full of stars. An owl glided close over our sleeping bags several times a night. Fish leaped. Tiny waves washed pebbles up and back. An unhurried, lingering dawn was suddenly clear bright sky. We found handfuls of good sticky clay and made some small bowls. After letting them bake dry in the sun for a couple of days, we fired them all day on the coals from our morning campfire in the sand. Nothing broke, nothing cracked. Every day we discovered small marvels.

BARBARA STROSS

Interstate 5, the freeway roughly paralleling the Willamette, is visible from Ross Island and only about two miles away. But even during the morning and afternoon rushes, traffic noises don't disrupt the solitude. Being on the island brings a lovely sense of detachment from events on shore. Every nuance of urban activity is in plain sight and easy earshot from midriver, but life here keeps its own pace and its pleasant privacy.

To the west and north of Ross Island, the landscape view is dominated by city buildings and streets. Due east, just across the river channel, Oaks Bottom remains protected from urban development. A natural floodplain for

139

the Willamette, it still has a year-round lake and numerous seasonal small ponds and marshes. A big culvert allows an interchange of water between Oaks Bottom and the Willamette, although reinforced riverbanks prevent annual flooding.

Oaks Bottom is a nice place to explore. The vegetation is mixed. Blackberries, English ivy, and clematis—all non-native species—have overgrown some areas almost completely. In others, the conifers, alders, black hawthornes, and wild crabapples are thriving. The city has approved a long-term planting plan that will eventually restore a native forest here. Almost every weekend between late fall and late spring, volunteer students and teachers from some of the local high schools clear brush, cut back the blackberries, and plant trees. In woodshop, students build bat boxes, like small wooden caves open on the underside, and hang them in the taller trees with good sun exposure. Since bats prefer to roost near a river or marsh, Oaks Bottom may very well house a colony in the future. A population of bats, which are insectivores with enormous appetites, near agricultural lands would significantly reduce the need for chemical pesticides on crops.

Oaks Bottom is home or feeding ground for quite a few interesting creatures. Blue herons and ducks on the lake and its marshy sidelands are nearly commonplace. Young carp, plentiful in this breeding ground, along with crappies, frogs, tadpoles, and salamanders, make fine food for herons. Other invertebrates and amphibians, including garter snakes and newts, can be found around the ponds in spring. Rabbits, field mice, possums, beavers, muskrats, raccoons, and occasionally mink, otters, coyotes, deer, and even a pair of bobcats share the territory. Birds and butterflies as well as squirrels are abundant. But residency is maintained exclusively for wildlife. Transients and homeless people who occasionally set up camps are quickly evicted when park caretakers find them.

A well-maintained trail traces the east side of Oaks Bottom, where a relatively steep bank along its entire length forms a natural enclosure. Several trails lead across to the west, which is bordered by the Willamette. An old railroad spur, still being used to haul lumber, is the north-south trail on this side.

With nearly 160 acres of protected land now being studied, maintained, and planted, Oaks Bottom is an exceptionally good habitat for urban wetland wildlife. Its proximity to Ross Island, a sanctuary much less susceptible to human impact (except where dredging continues), probably makes it more attractive to animals. Certainly anyone who loves the natural world will find more than enough things to see, do, and enjoy both on the island and in the marshes.

HOW TO GET THERE

To reach Sauvie, take Highway 30 toward Astoria. The well-marked turnoff for the Sauvie bridge is four miles beyond St. John's Bridge, on the outskirts of Portland. Ross, in the Willamette within the Portland city limits, is close enough to swim to, but we recommend launching a raft, boat, or bathtub as the current can be tricky.

CALIFORNIA

Angel Island

Want to get away for the day and feel like you've been away a week? Spend the day on this heavenly island in San Francisco Bay, a mere twenty-minute ride from San Francisco's ferry building or the dock in Marin County's Tiburon.

Bring your picnic, as many do, and frisbee for a day on the grass by the water at Ayala Cove, near the boat dock. In good weather, you can sunbathe on the beach there. The clarity of the water at Ayala is very unusual. The deep green, clear, calm bay reminds us of New Zealand; we half expect a kiwi to come scurrying out from the underbrush.

The undiscovered aspects of Angel Island are the many coves and trails and the historical buildings that exist beyond Ayala Cove. Stroll or bike the five-mile road that rings the island, or explore one of its hiking trails, which include a five-mile loop to the top of Mount Livermore and an unparalleled 360-degree view of the bay.

From the road and trails you will have vast views of the bay, its bridges, and surrounding cities, which are often shrouded in fog when the island itself rests in a pool of

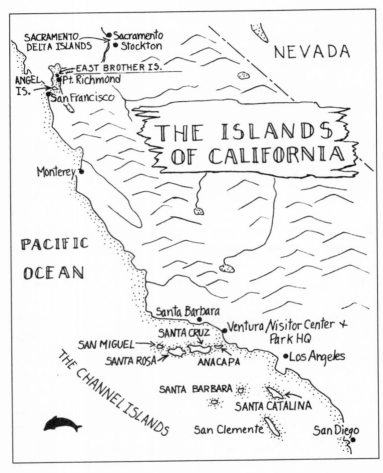

celestial sunlight. Several pleasant beaches are easily accessible from the ring road, which also makes an ideal bike ride. Bring your own bike or rent one in Tiburon.

You'll want to call at the visitor's center at Ayala Cove, just up from the ferry landing, to read about the history of the island and watch the instructive movie about its history, flora, and fauna. Trail maps and other information can be obtained from the ranger's office, located right on the boat dock.

Angel Island, the biggest island in San Francisco Bay, covers one square mile. It's name was anglicized from "Nuestra Señora de Los Angeles," the name bestowed by Lt. Juan Manuel de Ayala, the first European to anchor here.

The buildings around the island, many visible from the road, attest to its various historical uses. The most interesting is the Chinese Immigration Station. Although originally intended as an immigration station for Europeans arriving in this country through the Panama Canal, most of the immigrants detained here on the "Ellis Island of the West" from 1910 to 1940 were Chinese. Hopeful newcomers were held for up to a year in a prisonlike setting while their requests for immigration were processed. Approximately 175,000 Chinese immigrants came to the United States, "Gold Mountain," during that period, only to encounter restrictive anti-Asian laws, notably the Chinese Exclusion Act of 1882. Some tried to enter on false papers. About 10 percent of the detainees were deported, some of whom committed suicide rather than face a shameful return to their homeland.

At any one time, 200 to 300 men and 30 to 50 women were held in the cold, crowded building, which has largely been left untouched except for a photographic exhibit documenting the history of the Chinese on the West Coast. In the dormitory rooms you can still see Chinese poems that were carved into the wooden walls by the detainees. English renderings, along with the Chinese characters, are mounted on plain plaques under the fading testimonies.

I left my native village
to earn a living.
I endured wind and frost
to seek fame.
I passed this land to go to Cuba.
Who was to know
they would dispatch me to a prison on a mountain.

Sitting here,
uselessly delayed for long years and months,
my existing circumstances
justify my anger.
I am like a cuckoo in a cage.

Some 2,000 of those detained here have revisited the spot since its reopening as a landmark, a touching footnote to this onerous bit of largely unacknowledged history. Below the building, a monument has been erected by Vic Bergeron, owner of San Francisco's well-known restaurant, Trader Vic's. This site was also used to detain German and Japanese prisoners during World War II.

Angel Island, a very special piece of multiple-use real estate, has also been the site of the prisoner-cultivated kitchen gardens for neighboring Alcatraz, a quarantine station (this is why Ayala Cove is still referred to as Hospital Cove), and, remarkably, a dueling ground for San Franciscans. Ironically, one of the principals in the most famous of the duels fought here at Point Blunt was the author of California's anti-dueling law—U.S. Commissioner George Pen Johnston, whose rival, a state senator, lost his life in the confrontation.

Strategically located with a commanding view of the Golden Gate, the island has served many military purposes. Camp Reynolds, at West Garrison, was an army installation in continuous use from Civil War times to the end of World War II. More recently, a Nike missile site was located here, and parts of the island are still posted "off-limits." The island is now a state park.

LINDA LANCIONE MOYER

Angel Island was logged in the mid-nineteenth century, and to cover the ensuing barrenness, various non-native plants and trees were introduced, including pine, cypress, acacia, eucalyptus, and palm. In spring, the blue ceanothus, or "mountain lilac," is especially appealing. Any time of year, a sunny day on Angel Island provides a refreshing and invigorating escape from the city and a special perspective on San Francisco Bay.

A stroll around Tiburon is an added bonus to a day on Angel Island. There are several good restaurants on Main Street near the ferry dock. Main Street seems to dead-end at the Yacht Club but actually turns sharply and becomes a more interesting and sophisticated string of shops known as Ark Row. Some of the shops are in old remodeled arks in which people used to live when they were moored in Belvedere Cove. The first establishment on your right, at 72

Main Street, is the Tiburon Vintners, located in an old wooden building that was once a rooming house. At the entrance are two antique wine presses. Continuing along Ark Row, you'll find art galleries, clothing stores, a tiny but inviting deli, and at 116 Main Street, an Italian restaurant in an ark dated 1895. Main Street ends at Beach Road, where you'll have an excellent view of Belvedere Cove, tempting you to walk on and explore Corinthian Island and Belvedere Island, both peninsulas with elegant houses and hidden pedestrian paths. Less than half a mile uphill on Esperanza is old St. Hilary's, an example of "Carpenter's Gothic," defined as a simplified version of Gothic Revival architecture using locally available materials. The church, which was built in 1888, is also notable for its remarkable wildflower garden, St. Hilary's Preserve. Two hundred seventeen plant species have been identified on the four-acre site.

HOW TO GET THERE

Public ferries run to the island from San Francisco, Vallejo, and Tiburon daily June 1 through Labor Day. Tiburon Ferry runs Saturday and Sunday year-round and daily from June 1 through Labor Day.

From Tiburon, the ferry leaves on the hour from 10:00 a.m. to 3:00 p.m. on weekends. On weekdays, the boat leaves at 10:00 a.m., 1:00 p.m., and 3:00 p.m. The ride takes about 20 minutes. The fare is $5.00 for adults, $3.00 for children 5 to 18. This is "the only family-run ferry on the bay." To get to the ferry dock, take the Mill Valley/Tiburon exit off Highway 101 and follow the road to Tiburon.

The cheapest parking lot, $2.00, is on your left as you come into town. It's about a 15-minute walk to the dock.

Red and White Fleet Ferries depart from San Francisco (Ferry Building, foot of Market Street) and Vallejo Saturday and Sunday May through October, with additional service June 1 through Labor Day.

For further information on ferry schedules and fares, call the Angel Island-Tiburon Ferry at (415) 435-2131 or the Red and White Fleet, San Francisco, (800) 445-8880 or, from out of state, (415) 546-2896. During the off-season, schedules vary; call for current information.

If you wish to visit the island from November through May during the week, you must have your own boat. For private boaters, there are thirty mooring buoys at Ayala Cove and twenty at Quarry Beach.

WHERE TO STAY

There are only camping accommodations on the island itself. Reservations for overnight camping can be made by calling (800) 444-7275. The park has nine campsites in four areas, all with water and a pit toilet. Reservations can be made no earlier than eight weeks before the dates you want to camp, and you must bring a campstove or charcoal as no wood fires are allowed. Campsites are $7.00 off-season and $9.00 from April 1 through October 31.

Bed and Breakfast in Tiburon, 27 Old Landing Road, Tiburon, CA 94920, (415) 435-0605, is an ideal place for an overnight stay while visiting the island. Sandy Paul makes available one room with private bath in her woodsy, ranch-style home ten minutes from the ferry dock. There is a small beachfront across the street. Inexpensive/moderate.

Tiburon Lodge, 1651 Tiburon Boulevard, Tiburon, CA 94920, (415) 435-3133, also makes a good base from which to visit Angel Island. The ferry dock is only a ten-minute walk from here.

WHERE TO EAT

There's a snack bar on the island near the boat dock and a picnic area with barbecue pits at Ayala Cove, as well as numerous picnic tables with great views at other locations.

In Tiburon, three or four restaurants are located on the dock with terraces overlooking the bay, wonderful places to have breakfast before the ferry ride or dinner after. *Guaymas*, at 5 Main Street, is a stylish waterfront Mexican restaurant a few steps to your right as you disembark the ferry. The best bets here are the margaritas and the appetizer plate. The view of Angel Island, the Golden Gate Bridge, and San Francisco is unsurpassed. At 16 Main Street, you'll enjoy the best food in Tiburon at *Sasipim's*, a Thai restaurant decorated with gilded folk art. The smoky eggplant and *miang khum*, spinach leaves you fill at your table, are delicious. Open for lunch and dinner daily. A few steps west, at 38 Main Street, is *Rooney's Café and Grill*, where we liked the salads and daily lunch specials. The intimate little garden in back is the place for lunch on warm sunny days, and in this Bay Area "banana belt," this means nearly every day of the year.

CALIFORNIA

East Brother

One of the unexpected surprises of our enviable months of research for this book was the island that is smallest and closest to home, the East Brother Light Station, which we saved until last to visit. Although it is located in the San Pablo Strait, which connects San Francisco and San Pablo bays, this island is so undiscovered that even most native San Franciscans have never heard of it. Yet those who have stayed at its bed and breakfast describe it as a very romantic destination, and a day trip there rewards you with an extraordinary picnic site and a whole new slant on the bay.

The lighthouse, a three-story wooden building rather than the stereotypical cone, was built in 1873-74. In addition to the light itself, the building contained six rooms for three lighthousekeepers and their families. The station was manned continuously until 1969, when the Coast Guard automated the light and fog signal and closed the buildings. In 1979, a Coast Guard announcement of the planned destruction of the buildings came to the attention of Captain and Senior Officer Tom Edwards, who with his wife, Lucretia Edwards, a conservationist, got a group together to protest. With local architect Tom Butt, they formed East Brother Light Station Incorporated, a nonprofit organization that assumed responsibility for the restoration of the old building. After he read about their efforts in the newspaper, they were joined by Walter Fanning, who as a child had often stayed on the island visiting his grandfather, John Kofod, then the lighthousekeeper. In eight months of intense work, volunteers, aided by a $67,000 federal matching grant, restored the building, replacing the already

154

stripped original gingerbread, and made it ready for its rebirth as an inn.

The handsome buff-colored lighthouse, which operates Thursday through Sunday year-round as an inn, has white gingerbread trim, lace curtains, and two thriving rosebushes in front. Its porches, wide overhangs, and sawn bannisters, the details of which Walter Fanning helped reconstruct from memory, recall Victorian seaside cottages, but few such cottages have Mount Tamalpais and the

Richmond-San Rafael bridge in the background or views of the lights of San Francisco at night. The inn has four rooms plus a sitting room and dining room, all furnished in an early twentieth-century style. We particularly like the San Francisco room, with its subdued colors and view of the Richmond-San Rafael bridge. The $295.00 per night price per couple includes boat transportation from shore, breakfast, and a five-course dinner with wine. A peek at the guestbook reveals rave notices about the food, seconded by our food-savvy friends Joe and Shellie, owners of Point Richmond's Hidden City Café. Because the water supply on the island is limited to cistern-collected rain water, each room has a bathroom with toilet and basin but not all rooms have a shower. The profits from the inn go toward the expenses of continuing restoration.

The light, on the third floor, can by reached by visitors via an interior stairway. From October to April, a foghorn also sounds at close intervals from this spot; its position has been transferred from the top of the building, where it used to make things rattle, to a nearby site where its sound is more muffled.

Alicia and Denis Donovan, a friendly and unassuming young couple, are the current innkeepers. They do everything to make their guests comfortable, which is considerable, since they must haul everything—food, laundry, garbage—on and off the island themselves.

The innkeepers personally fetch and deliver guests from shore, a trip of about five minutes from the San Pablo Yacht Harbor, a hidden basin of funky boats and houseboats plus a small café. The trip does get rough sometimes; guests don't have time to get seasick but sometimes have to

seek protection from a soaking in the boat's tiny cabin. Only four guests are transported at a time, and only very rarely do the waters get so rough that the trip cannot be made. The boat passes by the last whaling station to close in California, in 1971. You can still see the wooden ramp where the whales were hauled up. On arrival, it is a climb up a six- or eight-rung ladder to the wharf.

If you can't manage a night out here, a day visit is an option. On Friday, Saturday, and Sunday, for a $10.00 per person fee (minimum four people), you can take the boat out to the island at 11:00 a.m. and return at 3:30 or 4:00 p.m. Picnic facilities, including barbecue and a horseshoe pit, are available.

East Brother Island, one acre in size, and its uninhabited companion rock, West Brother, are definitely for

BURL WILLES

bird lovers. They are among the few nesting places of the western gull, and baby gulls can be observed walking around here in June.

Some visitors fish off the wharf. Fanning remembers fishing here as a child for rock cod and perch as he watched the boats go by. In those days, he says, ''there were many sailing vessels still on the bay, as well as the stern-wheeled steamboats, *Delta King* and *Delta Queen*. The Monticello Steamship Company used to make their hourly San Francisco-Vallejo run.'' Fanning, who is a hale 82, heads up a team of volunteers who come to the island every Monday to work on the continuing restoration process. He has donated family antiques and photographs to the inn and speaks of its successful restoration, an accomplishment in which he played a large role, with quiet pride. "Of some fifty lighthouses on the California coast, one-third no longer exist or have been radically altered," says Fanning. He and his volunteer colleagues, through their imagination and energy, have found a creative way to finance this historic preservation and make it available to the public at the same time.

The hidden, historic community of Point Richmond, once an island itself, is only a short drive from the East Brother Island boat dock. Developer Jacob Tewksbury filled in the surrounding bay, and by 1904, the island became attached to what is now industrial Richmond.

Point Richmond remains an island in time. Early twentieth-century buildings have been beautifully restored around a central triangle where the new fire station, the library, a small history museum, and a colorful park are located. A walk around town only takes ten minutes, but don't rush. Stop and meet some of the locals and get a true sense of "life in the Point." Start at the fire station, where Jon Skaglund has painted a charmingly illustrated folk art street map at the corner of Park Place and West Richmond Avenue. Head north along Park Place. The old firehouse and the Baltic Restaurant (1910) are noteworthy buildings of decorated brick at 145 and 135 Park Place. The Baltic has an impressive "Old West" bar and a restful outdoor dining area. The Masquer's Theater (good local live productions) and Hidden City Café are a few steps farther along. Turn right on Washington Street and notice the fine restoration of 45 and 39 Washington Street and Edibles Catering at number 31. Across the street, the refurbished Hotel Mac (1908) is now a popular restaurant and bar.

Wave to octogenarian Hazel Ruby Carr, who sits regally in her ornately furnished red and gold real estate office at the corner of Cottage Street and Washington. That big, red, classic Imperial parked nearby belongs to Hazel. When this raven-haired lady is behind the wheel slowly circling the town triangle, there's no doubt that she is one of the Point's grande dames. Then step back in time at Sherry and Bob's Department Store at Washington and West Richmond Avenue, formerly the Bank of Richmond. Owner Sherry Hartynyk has been selling her merchandise since 1947. She'll be happy to show you her pièces de résistance, sequined evening dresses, from among the over-whelming amount of merchandise for sale.

In the library, next to the Indian statue and park, librar-ians Jo Bycraft and Jan Burdick will direct you to the latest issues of "This Point in Time," a monthly newsletter of the Point Richmond Historical Society which includes local residents' birthdays, all the latest gossip and trivia, and list-ings of town events as well as old photos and history. Next door is the history museum, housed in the town's oldest and smallest building, which was recently saved from the wrecking ball, hoisted on a dolly, and brought to this new site. Volunteer labor, old and young, continues to restore it inside and out. You'll have completed the tour when you've passed Lee's Flower Stand, the friendly Santa Fe Market, Ellie's Boarding House Reach Café, and Yoghurt and Espresso.

You can drive or walk up steep Washington Street, with its picturesque Victorian houses and churches. Linsley Hall (1904), the little brown shingle building on the left, once a church, is now a private residence. The owners rent

BURL WILLES

the garden and chapel for weddings. At the top of the hill
(¼ mile), there is a fine view of Mount Tamalpais, Marin
County, Angel Island, and all three bridges, Bay Bridge,
Golden Gate, and Richmond-San Rafael.

Follow Western Drive along the waterfront one-fourth
mile to Keller's Beach. The cold bay water doesn't seem to
deter the hardy locals. Bill Kollar, for one, has been swimming here since 1920.

Back on the town side of the hill through a short tun-
nel, the enormous indoor Point Richmond Plunge (built in
1926) is heated to a toasty 85 degrees. "My friend Danny
Keller and I were the first ones in the plunge on opening
day," Bill Kohler tells us. "They used half seawater, half
fresh then, and we stayed in the pool until closing time." To

swim, bring your bath towel and $1.75 for admission. There is no charge to walk along the upstairs observation gallery, from which you can see the pool in all its faded glory. A mural of the Taj Majal once covered the west wall, and when future restoration and seismic work are completed, the old mural will be replicated as closely as possible. Enjoy the plunge, but don't look for Bill; he's down at Keller's Beach, looking tan and healthy 65 years later.

Can a town like this really exist just fifteen miles from San Francisco? It can and it does. Hazel Ruby Carr will be the first to tell you it beats life in the fast lane with Howard Hughes.

HOW TO GET THERE

By public transportation: BART (Bay Area Rapid Transit) stops at El Cerrito del Norte station, 28 minutes by direct train from downtown San Francisco or 40 minutes from the Oakland Coliseum (with coach transfer to the Oakland Airport). Transfer at El Cerrito del Norte to the #72 bus, a 10-minute ride to Point Richmond or 12 minutes to Keller's Beach. BART trains run every 20 minutes, more often during commuting hours. AC Transit buses run every 30 minutes. There are taxis at both El Cerrito del Norte and Richmond stations for the drive to the East Brother boat dock at San Pablo Boat Harbor.

By car: Take the last exit, marked Point Molate, off Highway 880 at the west end of the Richmond-San Rafael bridge. Go left when the road forks, following the signs to Point Molate. Continue 2½ miles along the shoreline and through the village of Point Molate. Shortly after the tiny island and its lighthouse come into view, you will turn right and go up and over a hill, following the sign to the San Pablo Boat Harbor. Wait at the dock there for prearranged pickup. The inn supplies directions and a map to overnight guests.

WHERE TO STAY

East Brother Light Station Inc., 117 Park Place, Point Richmond, CA 94801, (415) 233-2385.

WHERE TO EAT

Dinner and breakfast are included in a stay at the lighthouse. Both are served in the common dining room around a handsome table.

Going and coming, you should try *Hidden City Café*, Park Place, Point Richmond. The locals know they have a real treasure in their neighborhood. Shellie Bourgault and Joe Branum were a success from the first week they opened in January 1990. Shellie trained at Berkeley's famous Chez Panisse, and her menu, which changes daily, includes a soup of the day, sandwiches, a daily pasta, and a daily special, all made with the freshest local ingredients. From soup to dessert, everything Shellie and Joe prepare is meticulous and consistently good. Hidden City is a true neighborhood café; white and blue collars, old and young, hip and unhip are regulars. Open 7:00 a.m. (wonderful breakfasts) to 3:00 p.m., closed Sunday and Monday. No reservations, no credit cards, and try to come early or late for lunch. Moderate.

The fine salad bar and sandwiches are not the main attraction at *Edibles*; it's the colorful garden—an inventive mixture of ferns, lavender, roses, heather, and vegetables.

Open 11:00 a.m. to 3:00 p.m. Closed Saturday and Sunday. Inexpensive.

Annie's friendly personality and engaging Korean-American accent have much to do with the success of the busy breakfast-lunch spot that bears her name. Soups, salads, and a daily special at very modest prices are the attraction. Annie's mom often gives a helping hand in the kitchen.

Time did not allow us to visit all the restaurants, but the *Hotel Mac* and the *Baltic*, both located in atmospheric historic buildings, are open for lunch and dinner.

The tiny café on the water at the *San Pablo Boat Harbor* is open 8:00 a.m. to 5:00 p.m. Wednesday through Sunday.

Sacramento Delta Islands

Just a short distance from the intense urban amalgam of the San Francisco Bay area, the Sacramento Delta is made up of many islands so closely linked by bridges and roads that we will treat them here as one island region. From the San Francisco Bay area, a leisurely loop by car can be made in an easy day that may include a meal overlooking the river, a stroll through a historical Chinese town, and a brief ferry ride.

The winding channels and austere marshland beauty of the Sacramento Delta's many islands—Ryer, Grand, Brannan, Andrus, Tyler, Sherman—remind us of the Netherlands. Only fifty miles from San Francisco, we suddenly found ourselves driving on dikes, beside water lower than the road. The flat fields extending as far as the eye can see,

the muted halftones, the fog, the drawbridges all evoked the lowlands of Europe. It's a giddy experience to drive along the levee road, seeing to one side, normally enough, the broad, placid Sacramento River and on the other side, the tops of mile after mile of Bartlett pear trees in bloom in their sunken orchards. The Sacramento Delta has a quiet beauty, unspectacular and timeless.

And the bird life! On the Pacific flyway, there are birds everywhere: blackbirds, marshhawks, white-tailed kites, coots. We saw an astonishing flock of white swans, hundreds and hundreds of them, right beside the road.

This is farm country. If you slow down to watch those swans, a pickup truck may swerve around you, horn blasting. There are pear orchards and apple orchards and tomatoes enough to paint the whole state in sauce Bolognese. It's comforting to find some of California's precious dwindling farmland so close to the city, where much of it has been given over to suburban development.

The watery twists and turns of the river and its tributaries yield up myriad recreation spots and offer a leisurely, tranquil meander by car. Probably the best way to see the Delta is by boat. You may want to take a turn behind the wheel of a houseboat (no previous piloting experience necessary). Sail, walk, or bike to appreciate the subtle and graceful charm of this unique region of California, with its leisurely pace and relaxed, unsophisticated life-style.

The vast maze of marshes and waterways that is the Delta is formed by the confluence of the Sacramento and San Joaquin rivers. Before the arrival of the Spanish, the Miwok ("people") made baskets, clothes, and huts from tule reed and lived from the bounty of river and land. After the arrival of the Spanish, the Indians fell under the control of the mission system. When Mexico attained independence from Spain, the dependent Indians were left to fend for themselves. Most were wiped out by an epidemic of malaria.

With the discovery of gold in Sacramento, steamboats transported miners and supplies to the newly booming city. The process of "reclaiming" the land for agriculture began in 1850, using Chinese laborers who had worked on the

SANDY McCULLOCH

transcontinental railroad. Their initial labor, done with hand tools, was accelerated when the clamshell dredge was developed, which made it possible to deepen the waterways and rapidly build up the levees with riverbottom mud.

Not all facets of land "reclamation" were positive. To facilitate a practice called riprapping, strengthening the levees with piles of stones, the Army Corps of Engineers systematically stripped the levees of trees and ground cover over a period of several years in the 1950s. The intervention of environmentalists resulted in a cessation of the practice and an attempt to refoliate the damaged areas that has fallen far short of total repair.

The Delta as it is today exists because of the levees. The islands are really polders. These mounds of riverbottom soil and gravel prevent not only flooding but the threat of any major construction development in the region, as the light soil is not stable enough to support the weight of much building. Water is both the bane and boon of the region. While its accessibility makes for easy agricultural irrigation, flooding poses an ever-present threat. In 1986, storms caused breaks in the levees and destruction of housing and marinas.

One of the most interesting aspects of the Delta is the Chinese presence here. Visit Locke, a one-street town with wooden sidewalks and a saloon straight out of an old western movie. The old Chinese gambling house is now a museum run by the Sacramento River Delta Historical Society. It's open 11:00 a.m. to 5:00 p.m. on weekends April through October. For a nominal admission fee, you can see displays of Pai Ngow, a game played with dominoes and

SANDY McCULLOCH

poker chips, Fan Tan, and other games of chance, as well as old photographs and clippings about the town's early days, and a collection of old ceramic water jugs and soy jars. The saloon in town is called Al's; on a recent Saturday evening, the bar was packed.

Other towns along the river were settlements for the levee builders, who included Japanese, Hawaiians, and Indians. Courtland is a sleepy place where the faces you see today are more likely to be Hispanic. Walnut Grove has little settlements on both sides of the river, to the east the old town and to the west a growing new community. Widely spaced in between the towns are handsome, well-painted farmhouses, some quite old looking.

In addition to its agriculture, the Delta is a serious recreation area. Many RV parks and funky cabin resorts are tucked away here, and little harbors such as Owl Harbor on Twitchell Bay offer berths for sailboats.

Spring, when the color is coming into the reeds and the fruit trees are flowering, is a lovely time here, as is fall, harvest time. Summers are hot, and November through January, the cold, unpleasant tule fog socks in the valley and makes driving dangerous.

"Far from the madding crowd," "a place where time stands still," and other clichés rattle about in your city-mind before it slows down enough to let in the calming vistas of water and marsh reed that lie about you. Once it does, we predict you will linger out here until the last light and return to the city with reluctance.

WHERE TO STAY

The Grand Island Inn (formerly Ryde Hotel), P.O. Box 43, Ryde, CA 95680, (916) 776-1318. Renovating in the style of an "art deco speakeasy," the new owners have made lemonade from this old lemon of a big, pink stucco building now done up in pink and gray with ceiling fans in the rooms and art deco posters. The large formal dining room has a fancy sounding menu with medium-priced entrées. Open from the first weekend in April through October, they do many special events such as weddings and serve private parties year-round. They have a New Year's Eve package that includes dinner, dancing to two bands, a room, and breakfast. Moderate.

The Delta Daze Inn, 20 Main Street, P.O. Box 607, Isleton, CA 95641, (916) 777-7777. A former gambling house and whorehouse located in Isleton's old Chinese section, the renovated old inn plus new addition has twelve rooms, all with private bath, television, and phone. A "Deltanental" breakfast of baked goods and fresh fruit is offered, with coffee in your room beforehand, if desired. At 4:00 p.m., snacks and soft drinks are made available, and guests are also served sodas and sundaes, included in the rate, at the "ice cream parlor." Moderate/expensive.

Brannan Island State Recreation Area has pleasant campsites along the water in stands of willow.

WHERE TO EAT

The Point is a Rio Vista restaurant located right on the water so you can watch the ships pass by as you eat. Their cargo and provenance is announced over the restaurant loudspeaker. Large portions of hamburgers, sandwiches, fish, and other standard American fare are served. *Das Cliffhaus*, an undistinguished-looking German restaurant on the riverbank, comes highly recommended for its *jaegersnitzel*.

In Isleton, both *Del Rio* and *Ernie's* serve steak and prime rib. Ernie's adds crawdads and deep-fried asparagus, and Del Rio a weekend country-western band. Up the scale is *La Croissanterie*, a good French restaurant. The most unusual restaurant in Isleton is *Rogelio's*, whose married proprietors, Mexican and Chinese, serve both cuisines.

Channel Islands

The southern California urban corridor—with its clogged freeways and its children who grow up saying they don't trust any air they can't see—steadily oozes its way up the California coast toward Santa Barbara. Meanwhile, some inspired decisions have ensured that the group of offshore islands in the Santa Barbara Channel remains pristine, the diverse and fascinating flora and fauna protected, the shapely silhouettes unchanged by human-made architecture save a lighthouse or two.

There are eight islands in the chain. In 1980, five of them—Santa Barbara, Santa Cruz, Santa Rosa, San Miguel, and Anacapa—along with six surrounding nautical miles of ocean were designated the Channel Islands National Park and National Marine Sanctuary. Today, the park is part of the International Man and the Biosphere program, whose goal is "to conserve genetic diversity and an environmental

LINDA LANCIONE MOYER

baseline for research and monitoring throughout the world." Of the remaining three islands, San Clemente and San Nicholas are owned by the U.S. government and used for military purposes. No visits are allowed. Santa Catalina, popularly referred to as "Catalina," is the best known island of the archipelago. The five islands that make up the national park are those usually referred to as the Channel Islands; however, we include Catalina since it is in fact one of the Channel Islands.

Channel Islands National Park

These channel islands are remote and difficult of access, but if you are in good physical condition, a visit to them,

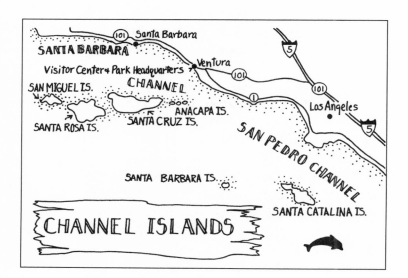

whether a day trip or overnight, can be extremely reward-ing. Each island has its own characteristics and habitat. Two private companies offer excursions to the islands: Island Packers runs boats from its moorings near the Visitors' Center in Ventura Harbor to all the park islands, while Channel Islands Adventures, based at the Camarillo airport, flies passengers on day and overnight trips to Santa Cruz and Santa Rosa islands. (See the How to Get There section below for details.)

The islands were first settled by the Chumash—or "island people"—Indians, who traveled back and forth in sturdy canoes to trade. In the early 1500s, Spanish and Por-tuguese explorers arrived on the islands. Gradually the Indians were removed to the mainland missions, replaced by ranchers from the mainland. In this century, the U.S. Coast Guard and the U.S. Navy have used parts of the islands for military purposes. Protection of the islands began under Franklin Roosevelt when, in 1938, he proclaimed Santa Barbara and Anacapa national monuments.

An hour spent at the park visitors center is an excellent introduction. Located in a handsome, weathered gray wood building at the harbor, it has a view of the islands on a clear day. Inside are displays of Indian artifacts, photos, and exhibits about the flora and fauna to be found on the islands. A twenty-five-minute film is shown frequently, and books and posters are available for purchase. Ask for free park service brochures about each island. The center is open seven days a week. Admission is free.

Anacapa

Anacapa, at eleven miles away the closest to shore, is really made up of three separate islands, inaccessible to each

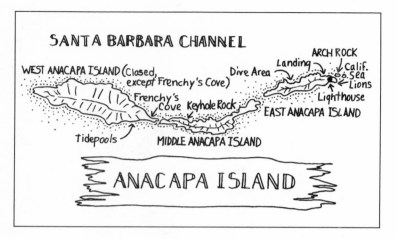

other except by boat. They consist of volcanic rock and lava ash. The erosion of wind and water results in unusual caves, terraces, and blowholes, most notably the spectacular Arch Rock, a forty-foot-high formation at the east end of the island.

Boat landings are made at East Anacapa via a six-passenger skiff that ferries from the larger boat to the landing place. From there, to visit the island, you must climb 153 stairs up the cliff. We were there in early April just after a heavy rain. The island stood in the sun-riddled mist wearing a stunning emerald green coat—a sight more expected off the Irish coast than the edge of California—but apparently it is brown and naked-looking most of the time. You will want to take a picnic and follow the 2.4-mile nature trail. Sometimes there is a ranger available to guide the hike and answer questions. There is an automated lighthouse and foghorn and some buildings that house park personnel. The park service warns that visitors near the foghorn risk damage to their hearing when it is in use.

LINDA LANCIONE MOYER

The slopes of West Anacapa are the primary nesting site for the western brown pelican. Access is forbidden to this part of the island to protect the rookery, except at Frenchy's Cove where the tide pools are noteworthy, as are the snorkeling and diving. There is a beach there, but access is only by private boat. Many sportfishing and scuba diving boats anchor there.

Santa Cruz

At 24 miles long, Santa Cruz is the largest of the island group. It is also the most diverse in landscape, with the highest mountain (Picacho Diablo, 2,434 feet) and a variety of steep cliffs, coves, caves, and sandy beaches. Painted Cave, 1,215 feet long, is the largest known sea cave in California. With ample fresh water, the island supports over 600 plant species. (There are 85 plant species endemic to the Channel Islands, of which 9 occur on Santa Cruz alone.) There are 140 land bird species to be found here, as

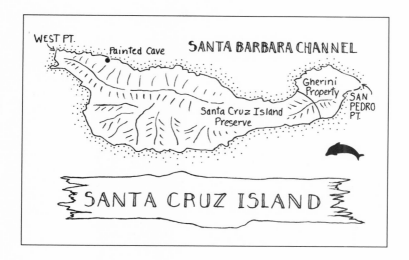

well as the island fox and other creatures that have adapted to the unique environment.

Santa Cruz Island is privately owned. In 1988, the Nature Conservancy acquired the western nine-tenths of the island, now managed as the Santa Cruz Island Preserve. The eastern end is scheduled for purchase by the National Park Service at some future unknown date. A permit is necessary for all boat landings. The Nature Conservancy conducts day trips to the island, and Island Adventures and Island Packers conduct recreational trips to the east end of the island.

Santa Rosa

This is the second largest island in the park group, also notable for its spectacularly varied terrain. A cattle ranch in the mid-nineteenth century, the cattle were replaced by

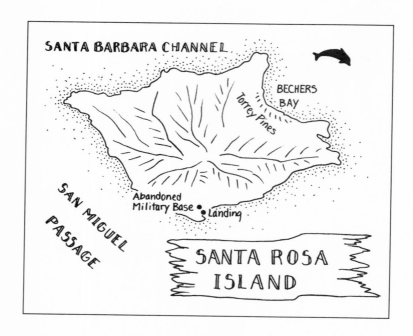

SANTA BARBARA CHANNEL

BECHERS
BAY

Torrey Pines

SAN MIGUEL PASSAGE

Abandoned
Military Base
Landing

SANTA ROSA
ISLAND

sheep after the California cattle industry collapsed, then by
cattle again. The combination of grazing and the introduction of nonnative grasses and animals severely damaged the
native plant communities of the island. Today, much of the
island is vast grassland, but there are also high mountains,
canyons, and columnar volcanic formations. Santa Rosa
supports a freshwater marsh that hosts many varieties of
birds and animal life. With over 195 species of birds, it is a
bird-watcher's paradise.

Birds and animals have not occupied the island alone.
There are over 160 archaeological sites; it can be shown
that the island was inhabited at least 8,000 years ago. There
is still a working cattle ranch on Santa Rosa Island today.

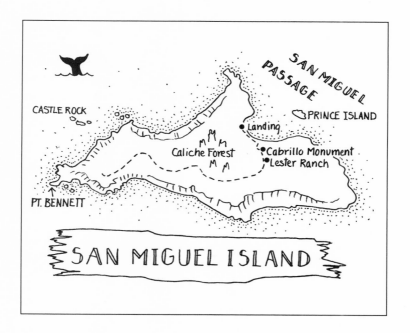

CASTLE ROCK

PRINCE ISLAND

Landing

Caliche Forest

Cabrillo Monument

Lester Ranch

PT. BENNETT

SAN MIGUEL ISLAND

San Miguel

This is the westernmost, therefore most remote, of the islands, and for the hardy, probably the most interesting. After a four-hour boat trip from the mainland, you reach a flat, windswept plateau with two rounded hills emerging from it. Unique to the island is the caliche "forest" that lies in the middle of it. Caliche is mineral sandcasting, which forms into unusual shapes. It's about a 3½-mile hike from the ranger's station at the top of the island to this unusual natural display. Most rewarding of all for experienced hikers is the 15-mile round-trip hike across the island to Point Bennett, from which you can see (at a one-mile distance) the breeding ground of thousands of seals and sea lions in their many varieties, including the gigantic, pre-historic-looking elephant seal with its enormous proboscis.

According to the park service, the Portuguese explorer Cabrillo may be buried on San Miguel. Although his grave has never been found, a monument overlooking Cuyler Harbor was erected in his memory in 1937.

Ranching began on the island in the 1850s, and a century later it was used for a decade as a bombing range. For that reason, adhering to marked trails is particularly important, as live ordnance still turns up occasionally.

Santa Barbara

Another breeding ground for elephant seals is Santa Barbara Island, the southernmost of the park islands. Five and one-half miles of nature trails lead through a landscape that is gradually being restored to its natural state after years of damage done by farming, grazing, and rabbits. The rabbits, not native to the island, have been removed, making it possible now for the attractive yellow daisy called coreopsis to grow ten feet high in spring.

HOW TO GET THERE

The two private companies that offer excursions to the Channel Islands are discussed above. Island Packers, which operates out of Ventura Harbor, does a variety of day and overnight boat trips to Anacapa, Santa Barbara, Santa Rosa, and San Miguel, depending on the season and the weather. For sunny weather and calm seas, the best time to go is September and October. The summer months are apt to be foggy, and spring winds make some landings difficult or impossible. The organization does not guarantee landing on the island destination. Indeed, we made an excursion to Anacapa only to discover that the swells were too high to allow the disembarking of a large load of passengers via the outboard-powered skiff that ferries from the larger boat to the landing place. We did watch one intrepid camper transported to the island this way despite the iffy conditions and were impressed with the care and caution exercised by the crew. When we commented afterward, they said, "One hurt finger could put us out of business."

Nevertheless, these trips and landings are not for the fainthearted. Among the warnings in Island Packers liter-

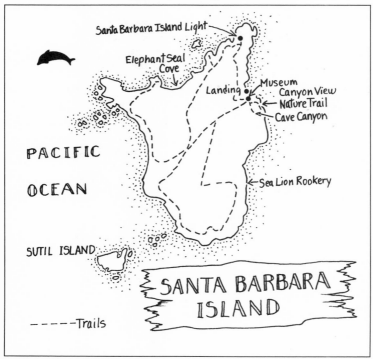

NATIONAL PARK SERVICE

ature: "Be physically and mentally prepared for possible 'Extra Excitement,'" and "Island landings are not for persons with heart conditions or restricted agility." For the seasick prone, Bonine or a similar product taken as directed works wonders, as does keeping your eyes focused on the horizon. The size and stability of the boats used varies; if you are in the area when you make your reservation, you might want to go down to the harbor to check out the boats yourself and talk to the crew before deciding which excursion is best for you. Island Packers, 1867 Spinnaker Drive, Ventura, CA 93001, (805) 642-1393.

Channel Island Adventures, 305 Durley Avenue, Camarillo, CA 93010, (805) 987-1678, flies to Santa Cruz Island for two-night stays at Christy Ranch and also offers a two-island day excursion to Santa Cruz and Santa Rosa.

Check with the park service for information about permits required for private boat landings. Each island has different regulations.

Recommended reading: *California's Channel Islands, 1001 Questions Answered*, by Marla Daily, (EZ Nature Books, 1990). This is available at the Visitor's Center.

WHERE TO STAY

Camping is permitted on Anacapa, Santa Barbara, and San Miguel islands. To obtain the necessary permit, call the Channel Islands National Park Visitor Center at (804) 644-8262 no more than ninety days in advance (30 days for San Miguel). The campgrounds can accommodate a maximum of thirty people per day. Campers must bring their own food, water, shelter, and cooking equipment and carry out all garbage. There are pit toilets. There is no shelter from sun or wind, which can be constant and ferocious. In other words, not only do you have to be in good condition but you have to really want to do this!

One- or two-night stays at *Scorpion Ranch* on the east end of Santa Cruz Island can be arranged through Island Packers. (See How to Get There.)

On Santa Cruz Island, Channel Islands Adventures offers two-night stays with meals provided at *Christy Ranch*, April through October.

Car campers who want to make day trips to the islands will find *McGrath State Park* in Ventura an agreeable campground. To reserve, call the state park reservation number at (800) 444-7275 no sooner than 56 days before your intended stay. For further information about the park, call (804) 654-4744.

For an elegant contrast to your rough-and-ready Channel Islands adventure, stay at *La Mer*, 411 Poli Street, Ventura, CA 93001, (805) 643-3600. This Victorian Cape Cod-style home, built in 1890, overlooks downtown Ventura and the ocean and is only a seven-minute drive from the harbor and a short walk to restaurants and the beach. The five rooms, with private entrances and private baths, are each decorated in the style of a different European country. The proprietor, Gisela Flender Baida, offers a Bavarian-style buffet breakfast and complimentary bottle of wine; she is happy to prepare a picnic for your boating excursion. Moderate/expensive.

WHERE TO EAT

On these Channel Islands, bring your own. *Lorenzoni's*, an espresso and sandwich shop near the Visitor's Center at the Ventura Marina, is happy to make up sandwiches to go, and they have excellent desserts and muffins, too. But go the night before or check to see if they're open before your boat departure time (tel. 654-0546).

Another sandwich and/or breakfast option is *Christy's*, also at the Ventura Marina, open 7:00 a.m. to 3:00 p.m. seven days a week.

Nearby is *Andria's*, which might be the ultimate place to have dinner the night before a strenuous boat ride. This noisy, friendly, extremely casual place serves up huge portions of fish and chips and their variations, very cheap. We even saw them cooking up an individual portion of cioppino in an ancient frying pan. There are other restaurants in this same commercial complex.

In downtown Ventura, try *Chez Kim* for French flavor, *Tipps Thai* for fine Thai food, or the *Rosarito Beach Café* for fresh Mexican food with a seafood emphasis.

A few miles farther south at the Channel Islands Harbor in Oxnard is another pleasant complex of shops and restaurants. Our favorite budget choice was *Channel Islands Harbor Seafood Company*, a combination fish market and take-out fish restaurant. We ordered a pound of shrimp from the market and paid an extra $1.00 to have them steamed. That plus some clam chowder and an order of French bread and a couple of beers was dinner for three for under $20.00. There are outdoor tables where you can people-watch and catch an occasional jazz band on summer weekends.

Santa Catalina

Catalina? Undiscovered? Oh, come on. Everyone knows about Catalina. But have you ever been to this splendid slice of the Mediterranean off the southern California coast, this Capri-before-the-tourists-found-it? Avalon, the main town, with its restaurants, souvenir shops, winding streets, appealing houses, and spectacular views, is like a half dozen California beach towns all rolled into one. Most people stream into charming Avalon for a day or a weekend and return to the mainland ignorant of the 99 percent of Catalina that is still undiscovered.

Instead, go to Two Harbors, the tiny settlement at the west end of the island where the land narrows to a half-

LINDA LANCIONE MOYER

mile-wide isthmus. A clutch of makeshift buildings along the palm- and eucalyptus-lined shore makes you think you've arrived at an outpost 4,000 miles out in the Pacific—Fantasy Island maybe?—instead of being only one and a half hours away from the gray grit of the Los Angeles freeways. We were there in April after a heavy rain; the hills were green, the air was tropically moist, and lupine and yellow daisies were in bloom among the cactus.

The two harbors for which the town is named— Catalina Harbor and Isthmus Cove—flank the isthmus. Catalina Harbor is where the ferries come in; on the other side, at Isthmus Cove, there is a yacht club and boat moorings. On a summer weekend "the isthmus," as this part of the island is known by the locals, rocks with sailboat traffic, but off-season, it's a tranquil idyll of fresh air, slow walks, and water play. For example, you can hike six miles

BURL WILLES

to Emerald Bay, where there is a sandy beach, warmer water than at Two Harbors, and foliage that comes right down to the bay. Or rent diving equipment at the Two Harbors Dive Shop. It's an ideal spot for photography or sketching or bird-watching or just lying in the grass and listening to the crickets. At night you can see the twinkling lights of the Los Angeles coast, but the sound of the freeway doesn't reach this far.

Two Harbors is described as a company town; you can only live there if you work for Doug Bombard Enterprises, proprietors of virtually everything in the town, including Banning House and the campground. Bombard leases the land from the Catalina Island Company. There is a restaurant, a snack bar, a general store, the dive shop, and not much else. The oldest building, once the barracks of Union soldiers during the Civil War, is now a yacht club.

The only hotel option is lovely Banning House Lodge, situated on a knoll with views in all directions, well away from the minor hurly-burly of the town. Its broad veranda, dark paneled living room, and airy chintz and wicker sun porch are so attractive you may not wish to leave the premises. Hosts Ian and Maryann are relaxed, cordial people who love working on the island. They even do all the cooking on nights when dinner is served here.

The campground at Two Harbors is also very well sited, a short walk from the boat landing but still a protected distance from the town. The sites are scattered over a hill sloping down to the beach, well spaced, and protected from the sun by thatched roofs. There is a plan to install tent cabins in 1991.

If you really want to get away from it all, the ideal place to camp is at Little Harbor, on the coast seven miles from Two Harbors (the bus that runs from Two Harbors to Avalon will drop you there). There are lovely campsites situated on a splendid beach.

Near Two Harbors is USC's Marine Institute, a field station for university research. The institute is best known for its hyperbaric chamber in which the victims of diving accidents can be decompressed. With advance notice of at least a week, tours of the institute can be arranged for a minimum of fifteen people. Call (213) 510-0811.

Catalina has had a motley series of occupants since Juan Cabrillo first discovered it in 1542. With the arrival of the Spanish in the 1500s, the Indian population died off (a familiar story). In addition to the Spanish and the Indians, Russian fur traders, slave traders, miners, Civil War soldiers, and movie makers have all lived here. In 1919, the island was purchased by the Wrigley chewing gum family. The

BURL WILLES

population of the island now is 2,500, about the same number it supported when only Indians lived here.

Eighty-six percent of Catalina, most of the island outside of Avalon and Two Harbors, is now owned by the Catalina Conservancy, a gift from the Wrigley family, whose purpose is to ensure that its holdings remain undeveloped and in their natural state. The Conservancy maintains one hundred miles of roads and trails, as well as a visitor's center and native plant nursery at the airport.

You can come and go from Two Harbors by ferry without visiting the busy end of the island, but the 26-mile road across the island to Avalon is certainly spectacular. Catalina Safari runs a bus or van, depending on the demand, once or twice daily. The cost is $14.50, and reservations are necessary. The road is narrow and only paved part of the way, with some extremely interesting hairpin turns toward the Avalon side. The drive, which takes one and a half hours, is considerably shorter than the two and a half days it used to take by stagecoach. The views of the mountains, ravines, and coves that make up the island are magnificent, and you may glimpse the wild bison, burrowing owls, wild goats, channel fox, and other wildlife that the island is home to. The bus drives through Rancho Escondido, Wrigley home to 700 prize Arabian horses, and the Airport-in-the-Sky, which serves commercial and private planes.

A ride across the island reveals its astonishing steep canyons and palisades and glimpses of the delectable coves and boat moorings tucked along the coast. The rugged terrain, combined with the ocean climate and isolation from shore, have all contributed to the development of an ecosystem distinctive from that of the mainland. Plant species no longer found on the mainland grow here, and 8 of the island's 396 native plants grow *only* here. These include the Catalina mahogany, Catalina ironwood, and St. Catherine's lace. One of the ironwood groves is located east of Banning Lodge at Two Harbors.

Some problematic species found here are not native to the island. The Spanish brought goats, which defoliated the once lush island. The Conservancy is working toward their elimination. Management of another imported animal continues to be a question; the bison brought here for the filming of one of Zane Grey's novels and left to roam wild have occasionally attacked humans who have interfered with them. Obviously, they should not be approached.

The interior of the island is a hikers' and backpackers' paradise because of the temperate climate, the well-made trails, the isolated campsites, and the many coves and inlets to be discovered. However, hikers frequently encounter rattlesnakes and poison oak. A detailed trail map and visitors guide is for sale on the island or may be obtained from the Catalina Conservancy, P.O. Box 2739, Avalon, CA 90704.

Though hardly undiscovered, the town of Avalon, named after a place in Tennyson's poem, "The Idylls of the King," is worth a day of exploration. To get away from the bustling waterfront, take an early morning walk (two miles from the beach) past the golf course to the botanical garden, which is full of native and Mediterranean plants. The garden is at the base of a massive memorial to Wrigley that towers over the valley. We couldn't help think that a subtle Buddhist temple blending in with the landscape, or even a terrace restaurant, would have better enhanced the splendid site.

The management seems happy to have you look around the Zane Grey Pueblo, now a hotel, even if you don't want to stay there. The novelist spent most of his later years here, fishing and writing, and each room is now named after one of his novels. High on a hill overlooking the town and harbor, this locale would give inspiration to any writer.

Way across the harbor on the hills opposite is the elegant Wrigley mansion, now the Inn at Mount Ada, which offers tours to the public at noon every day but Monday and Saturday and otherwise remains behind locked gates for the exclusive use of its guests.

The landmark round casino that Wrigley had built in 1929 at one end of the harbor is now used as a ballroom and movie theater. It houses a museum with artifacts from Catalina's history. Free admission.

Cars are not permitted on the island, but bicycles and little golf cart-like cars are available for rental on a first come, first served basis, for use in and around Avalon only. The car rentals were $25.00 per hour when we were there. You must be 25 or older and show a current driver's license to rent them. Bikes are $5.00 per hour ($10.00 for a tandem bike). Bike permits for other parts of the island cost $50.00 per person or $75.00 per couple (this high because of insurance rates, we were told) for the season. In October, one of us rented a boat and motored along the coast to hidden coves and snorkeled in water so clear you could see twenty feet to the bottom.

Catalina, especially Two Harbors, reminded us of other places. The color of the water, the bright geraniums, and the palm trees recall the French Riviera, and the dry reddish earth and the rocky paths that curve around the coastline from the harbors made us think of islands in Greece. Our friend Meredith even said the clear dry air reminded her of the ranch she grew up on in Placerville, but the air is not so dry that after a spring rain you don't think a little of the dark, forested palis of Hawaii as well. It's a lovely place, and we're glad it is protected from further growth and is available to everyone who can make the crossing.

HOW TO GET THERE

By boat: Boats leave from the Los Angeles Harbor at San Pedro, from Long Beach, and from Redondo Beach and Newport Beach. There are two boat companies, Catalina Cruises and Catalina Express. From San Pedro, Catalina Express (213/519-1212) charges around $29.00 and takes one and a half hours. Catalina Express is developing a hydrofoil that will make the trip in 45 minutes. Boats to Avalon run several times a day; some also go to Two Harbors. This company also serves Long Beach and Redondo Beach. Catalina Cruises departs only from Long Beach. Call (213) 253-9800 or (800) 888-5939 for schedules and fares. There is also daily service from the Balboa Pavilion in Newport Beach (714/673-5245).

To get to the San Pedro Harbor from Los Angeles, take the Harbor Freeway (110) South to the Harbor Boulevard Exit (also clearly marked Catalina), go straight ahead at the intersection and park in the 5-Star Parking Lot, which has an attendant on duty. The cost is $5.50 per day.

By air: There is helicopter service from San Pedro's Catalina Island Terminal (213/548-1314 or 800/262-1472).

Island Express (213/491-5550) flies from San Pedro and Long Beach in about 20 minutes. Allied Charter Air (213/510-1163) schedules commuter runs from Long Beach Airport and John Wayne Airport in Orange County.

WHERE TO STAY

Banning House Lodge, Box 5044, Two Harbors, CA 90704-5044, (213) 831-2CAT for reservations and (213) 510-2800 for information and group services. The hospitable Banning House Lodge has twelve rooms, many with splendid views. They are open all year. Situated on a knoll above Two Harbors, it peacefully surveys both bays. Banning House was built by a shipping and stagecoach family who used it as their summer and party house. It has a handsome wood-paneled living room, a charming wicker-and-chintz sun porch, a large sheltered veranda, and a couple of decks with Adirondack chairs. A continental breakfast is served on pretty floral china in the lace-curtained dining room. Our favorite room, called the Crow's Nest, has a little balcony that looks out over the harbor.

The *campground at Two Harbors* is run through Banning House Lodge. For other camping options, call *Catalina Cove and Camp* at (213) 510-0303 or *Los Angeles County* at (213) 510-0688.

Of the many hotels in Avalon, we have chosen three for their diversity and special character.

The Inn on Mt. Ada, 1 Wrigley Road, Avalon, Catalina, CA 90704, (213) 510-2030. Formerly the Wrigley mansion, this elegant place, which one writer describes as a "white wedding cake," perches high above the harbor. It is quietly and tastefully decorated and noted for its privacy and discreet attentive service, which includes breakfast, tea, and hors d'oeuvres. There are only six bedrooms, all with private baths. It was described to us by one world traveler as one of the most exquisite places she had ever stayed. Expensive.

Zane Grey Hotel, P.O. Box 216, Avalon, CA 90704, (213) 510-0966. Splendidly situated above Avalon, the former home of this prolific writer, built in 1926, is now a hotel with fourteen rooms. Half of the rooms have ocean views, half have views of the mountains. All are furnished in a simple Southwest style, some with original western landscape paintings by Bud Upton. The hotel has a small swimming pool, and the grand piano in the living room is available to the guests. Inexpensive/moderate.

La Paloma, P.O. Box 1505, Avalon, CA 90704, (213) 510-0737. Up a side street in Avalon, so it's both quiet and centrally located, this rustic hotel dating from the 1920s consists primarily of rows of housekeeping cottages that flank a long trellised brick staircase that extends up a slope between two streets. When we were there in April, the wisteria overhanging the stairs was in bloom and the carefully tended patches of garden on either side of the stairs made us feel we were somewhere in Italy or France. The units are small and charmless but very clean, and the garden, location, and hospitality of the managers are all excellent. Inexpensive/moderate.

WHERE TO EAT

There is one restaurant and snack bar at Two Harbors; the snack bar closes in the afternoon.

The restaurant, *Doug's Harbor Reef and Saloon*,

serves such things as chicken teriyaki, steak with shrimp, and fresh fish. The baby back ribs and the prime rib were highly recommended by the locals. Dinners run from $14.00 to $19.00. Reservations are essential in the summer. The restaurant is closed Thanksgiving through Presidents' Day and Monday through Wednesday through the spring.

When the restaurant is closed, *Banning House Lodge* serves dinner to its guests and will take reservations from nonguests. Call at least by the morning of the dinner. Cooking is done by the host or hostess, Ian or Marianne, as if for one big dinner party, so there is no choice of menu. The cost is $16.95 per person.

Among the many restaurants in Avalon, *Armstrong's*, in the center of town right on the water, is highly recommended for its fish. *Prego*, on the main street just where you turn to go out on the pier where the boats come in, has hearty Italian fare. For a $5.00 surcharge, they arrange for you to split a pasta dinner and have a salad each instead of the soup and salad that comes with a single dinner. On the road to the botanical garden, across from the golf course, is *Silky's*, which serves lunch and dinner in an elegant country club courtyard. We didn't get a chance to eat there, but more than one local person recommended it. Rumor has it that the building is to be torn down, which would be a shame as it's a very pretty piece of old California/Spanish-style architecture.

Other Books from John Muir Publications

Adventure Vacations: From Trekking in New Guinea to Swimming in Siberia, Bangs 256 pp. $17.95

Asia Through the Back Door, 3rd ed., Steves and Gottberg 326 pp. $15.95

Belize: A Natural Destination, Mahler, Wotkyns, Schafer 304 pp. $16.95

Buddhist America: Centers, Retreats, Practices, Morreale 400 pp. $12.95

Bus Touring: Charter Vacations, U.S.A., Warren with Bloch 168 pp. $9.95

California Public Gardens: A Visitor's Guide, Sigg 304 pp. $16.95

Catholic America: Self-Renewal Centers and Retreats, Christian-Meyer 325 pp. $13.95

Costa Rica: A Natural Destination, Sheck 280 pp. $15.95 (**2nd ed.** available 3/92 $16.95)

Elderhostels: The Students' Choice, 2nd ed., Hyman 312 pp. $15.95

Environmental Vacations: Volunteer Projects to Save the Planet, Ocko 240 pp. $15.95 (**2nd ed.** available 2/92 $16.95)

Europe 101: History & Art for the Traveler, 4th ed., Steves and Openshaw 372 pp. $15.95

Europe Through the Back Door, 9th ed., Steves 432 pp. $16.95 (**10th ed.** available 1/92 $16.95)

Floating Vacations: River, Lake, and Ocean Adventures, White 256 pp. $17.95

Great Cities of Eastern Europe, Rapoport 240 pp. $16.95

Gypsying After 40: A Guide to Adventure and Self-Discovery, Harris 264 pp. $14.95

The Heart of Jerusalem, Nellhaus 336 pp. $12.95

Indian America: A Traveler's Companion, Eagle/Walking Turtle 448 pp. $17.95

Mona Winks: Self-Guided Tours of Europe's Top Museums, Steves and Openshaw 456 pp. $14.95

Opera! The Guide to Western Europe's Great Houses, Zietz 296 pp. $18.95

Paintbrushes and Pistols: How the Taos Artists Sold the West, Taggett and Schwarz 280 pp. $17.95

The People's Guide to Mexico, 8th ed., Franz 608 pp. $17.95

The People's Guide to RV Camping in Mexico, Franz with Rogers 320 pp. $13.95

Ranch Vacations: The Complete Guide to Guest and Resort, Fly-Fishing, and Cross-Country Skiing Ranches, 2nd ed., Kilgore 396 pp. $18.95

The Shopper's Guide to Art and Crafts in the Hawaiian Islands, Schuchter 272 pp. $13.95

The Shopper's Guide to Mexico, Rogers and Rosa 224 pp. $9.95

Ski Tech's Guide to Equipment, Skiwear, and Accessories, ed. Tanler 144 pp. $11.95

Ski Tech's Guide to Maintenance and Repair, ed. Tanler 160 pp. $11.95

A Traveler's Guide to Asian Culture, Chambers 224 pp. $13.95

Traveler's Guide to Healing Centers and Retreats in North America, Rudee and Blease 240 pp. $11.95

Understanding Europeans, Miller 272 pp. $14.95

Undiscovered Islands of the Caribbean, 2nd ed., Willes 232 pp. $14.95

Undiscovered Islands of the Mediterranean, Moyer and Willes 232 pp. $14.95

Undiscovered Islands of the U.S. and Canadian West Coast, Moyer and Willes 208 pp. $12.95

A Viewer's Guide to Art: A Glossary of Gods, People, and Creatures, Shaw and Warren 144 pp. $10.95

2 to 22 Days Series

Each title offers 22 flexible daily itineraries that can be used to get the most out of vacations of any length. Included are not only "must see" attractions but also little-known villages and hidden "jewels" as well as valuable general information.

22 Days Around the World, 1992 ed., Rapoport and Willes 256 pp. $12.95
2 to 22 Days Around the Great Lakes, 1992 ed., Schuchter 192 pp. $9.95
22 Days in Alaska, Lanier 128 pp. $7.95
2 to 22 Days in the American Southwest, 1992 ed., Harris 176 pp. $9.95
2 to 22 Days in Asia, 1992 ed., Rapoport and Willes 176 pp. $9.95
2 to 22 Days in Australia, 1992 ed., Gottberg 192 pp. $9.95
22 Days in California, 2nd ed., Rapoport 176 pp. $9.95
22 Days in China, Duke and Victor 144 pp. $7.95
2 to 22 Days in Europe, 1992 ed., Steves 276 pp. $12.95
2 to 22 Days in Florida, 1992 ed., Harris 192 pp. $9.95
2 to 22 Days in France, 1992 ed., Steves 192 pp. $9.95
2 to 22 Days in Germany, Austria & Switzerland, 1992 ed., Steves 224 pp. $9.95
2 to 22 Days in Great Britain, 1992 ed., Steves 192 pp. $9.95
2 to 22 Days in Hawaii, 1992 ed., Schuchter 176 pp. $9.95
22 Days in India, Mathur 136 pp. $7.95
22 Days in Japan, Old 136 pp. $7.95
22 Days in Mexico, 2nd ed., Rogers and Rosa 128 pp. $7.95
2 to 22 Days in New England, 1992 ed., Wright 192 pp. $9.95
2 to 22 Days in New Zealand, 1991 ed., Schuchter 176 pp. $9.95
2 to 22 Days in Norway, Sweden, & Denmark, 1992 ed., Steves 192 pp. $9.95
2 to 22 Days in the Pacific Northwest, 1992 ed., Harris 192 pp. $9.95
2 to 22 Days in the Rockies, 1992 ed., Rapoport 176 pp. $9.95
2 to 22 Days in Spain & Portugal, 1992 ed., Steves 192 pp. $9.95
22 Days in Texas, Harris 176 pp. $9.95
22 Days in Thailand, Richardson 176 pp. $9.95
22 Days in the West Indies, Morreale and Morreale 136 pp. $7.95

Parenting Series

Being a Father: Family, Work, and Self, *Mothering* Magazine 176 pp. $12.95
Preconception: A Woman's Guide to Preparing for Pregnancy and Parenthood, Aikey-Keller 232 pp. $14.95
Schooling at Home: Parents, Kids, and Learning, *Mothering* Magazine 264 pp. $14.95
Teens: A Fresh Look, *Mothering* Magazine 240 pp. $14.95

"Kidding Around" Travel Guides for Young Readers

Written for kids eight years of age and older.

Kidding Around Atlanta, Pedersen 64 pp. $9.95
Kidding Around Boston, Byers 64 pp. $9.95
Kidding Around Chicago, Davis 64 pp. $9.95
Kidding Around the Hawaiian Islands, Lovett 64 pp. $9.95
Kidding Around London, Lovett 64 pp. $9.95
Kidding Around Los Angeles, Cash 64 pp. $9.95
Kidding Around the National Parks of the Southwest, Lovett 108 pp. $12.95
Kidding Around New York City, Lovett 64 pp. $9.95
Kidding Around Paris, Clay 64 pp. $9.95
Kidding Around Philadelphia, Clay 64 pp. $9.95
Kidding Around San Diego, Luhrs 64 pp. $9.95
Kidding Around San Francisco, Zibart 64 pp. $9.95
Kidding Around Santa Fe, York 64 pp. $9.95
Kidding Around Seattle, Steves 64 pp. $9.95
Kidding Around Spain, Biggs 108 pp. $12.95
Kidding Around Washington, D.C., Pedersen 64 pp. $9.95

Environmental Books for Young Readers
Written for kids eight years and older.

The Indian Way: Learning to Communicate with Mother Earth, McLain 114 pp. $9.95
The Kids' Environment Book: What's Awry and Why, Pedersen 192 pp. $13.95
Rads, Ergs, and Cheeseburgers: The Kids' Guide to Energy and the Environment, Yanda 108 pp. $12.95

"Extremely Weird" Series for Young Readers
Written for kids eight years of age and older.

Extremely Weird Bats, Lovett 48 pp. $9.95
Extremely Weird Frogs, Lovett 48 pp. $9.95
Extremely Weird Primates, Lovett 48 pp. $9.95
Extremely Weird Reptiles, Lovett 48 pp. $9.95
Extremely Weird Spiders, Lovett 48 pp. $9.95

Quill Hedgehog Adventures Series
Written for kids eight years of age and older. Our new series of green fiction for kids follows the adventures of Quill Hedgehog and his Animalfolk friends.

Quill's Adventures in the Great Beyond. Waddington-Feather 96 pp. $5.95
Quill's Adventures in Wasteland, Waddington-Feather 132 pp. $5.95
Quill's Adventures in Grozzieland, Waddington-Feather 132 pp. $5.95

Other Young Readers Titles

Kids Explore America's Hispanic Heritage, edited by Cozzens 112 pp. $7.95 (avail. 2/92)

Automotive Repair Manuals

How to Keep Your VW Alive, 14th ed., 440 pp. $21.95
How to Keep Your Subaru Alive 480 pp. $21.95
How to Keep Your Toyota Pickup Alive 392 pp. $21.95
How to Keep Your Datsun/Nissan Alive 544 pp. $21.95

Other Automotive Books

The Greaseless Guide to Car Care Confidence: Take the Terror Out of Talking to Your Mechanic, Jackson 224 pp. $14.95
Off-Road Emergency Repair & Survival, Ristow 160 pp. $9.95

Ordering Information
If you cannot find our books in your local bookstore, you can order directly from us. Please check the "Available" date above. If you send us money for a book not yet available, we will hold your money until we can ship you the book. Your books will be sent to you via UPS (for U.S. destinations). UPS will not deliver to a P.O. Box; please give us a street address. Include $3.25 for the first item ordered and $.50 for each additional item to cover shipping and handling costs. For airmail within the U.S., enclose $4.00. All foreign orders will be shipped surface rate; please enclose $3.00 for the first item and $1.00 for each additional item. Please inquire about foreign airmail rates.

Method of Payment
Your order may be paid by check, money order, or credit card. We cannot be responsible for cash sent through the mail. All payments must be made in U.S. dollars drawn on a U.S. bank. Canadian postal money orders in U.S. dollars are acceptable. For VISA, MasterCard, or American Express orders, include your card number, expiration date, and your signature, or call (800) 888-7504. Books ordered on American Express cards can be shipped only to the billing address of the cardholder. Sorry, no C.O.D.'s. Residents of sunny New Mexico, add 5.875% tax to the total.

Address all orders and inquiries to:
John Muir Publications
P.O. Box 613
Santa Fe, NM 87504
(505) 982-4078
(800) 888-7504